W9-BSB-236

Found in the Middle!

Found in the Middle!

Theology and ethics for
Christians who are both liberal
and evangelical

WESLEY J. WILDMAN

STEPHEN CHAPIN GARNER

Herndon, Virginia
www.alban.org

The Alban Institute

2121 Cooperative Way, Suite 100

Herndon, VA 20171

Unless otherwise noted, all Scripture quotations are from the New Revised Standard Version of the Bible, copyright © 1989, Division of Christian Education of the National Council of the Churches of Christ in the United States of America, and are used by permission.

Scripture quotations marked KJV are from the King James Version of the Bible.

Scripture quotations noted NIV are from Holy Bible: New International Version, copyright © 1973, 1978, 1984. Used by permission of Zondervan Bible Publishers.

Scripture quotations noted TNIV are from Today's New International® Version TNIV©. Copyright 2001, 2005 by International Bible Society®. Used by permission of International Bible Society®. All rights reserved worldwide.

Cover design by Spark Design.

Library of Congress Cataloging-in-Publication Data

Wildman, Wesley J., 1961-
 Found in the middle! : theology and ethics for Christians who are both liberal and evangelical / Wesley J. Wildman, Stephen Chapin Garner.
  p. cm.
 Includes bibliographical references.
 ISBN 1-56699-381-4
 1. Liberalism (Religion)--Protestant churches. 2. Evangelicalism. 3. Theology--Popular works. 4. Christian ethics. I. Garner, Stephen Chapin, 1969- II. Title.
 BR1615.W55 2009
 277.3'083--dc22

                        2009000370

09 10 11 12 13   VP   5 4 3 2 1

In honor of Phillip Charles Wildman,
provider and supporter, father and friend.

In memory of my father, Stephen Elwood Garner,
the man I still hope to grow up to be like.

Contents

PART II. GOD WAS IN CHRIST

PART III. CHOOSING THE SUGAR-SHACK CHURCH

Preface

We wrote our previous book, *Lost in the Middle?* for Christians who feel theologically and spiritually displaced. They feel lost in the middle between the noisy extremes of religion and politics and long to feel at home there instead. We presented the demographic, political, existential, sociological, and historical perspectives that help such Christians confidently set aside the oversimplifications of left and right and go deep instead. That book recounted the noble heritage of Christians who uphold the highest values of liberalism and evangelicalism simultaneously. It helped them feel at home in the middle by explaining why they feel lost there and introducing them to their lineage in the Christian faith.

This book, *Found in the Middle!*, focuses on the problems that arise when Christians of this passionately moderate sort find each other and gather together in congregations. Their churches intentionally aim to model for the world a kind of community that rises above territorial instincts and insults, one that stresses love and acceptance more than cultural identity and security. But that is no easy calling. It is bracing to worship beside someone with a completely opposite view on legal access to abortion or on economic and taxation policy, to know that you disagree, and yet still to find love and acceptance together at the Communion table. But sooner or later you have to talk meaningfully with your political and ethical opponent, whom you strive to love and respect. Your church needs a theological and ethical self-understanding that everyone can sign on to or it will pull apart. Having a shared determination to stay together no matter what is a good start, but it is not enough.

Some say it is enough if people worship together. Based on our own experience and drawing on considerable research into congregations, we disagree. Worship functions as vital glue for keeping moderate Christians together in face of the stresses of disagreement. But the preached message matters just as much. If sermons and education do not help people talk confidently about their faith to each other and to those beyond the borders of their community, then worshipful togetherness will never survive the ordinary trials of disagreement. If an intentional community cannot have a vision of Christian good news in common, then their corporate faith risks becoming a formless muddle briefly masquerading as joyful pluralism.

To put the matter in another way, moderate Christians in intentionally pluralistic communities of faith discover sooner or later that togetherness only works when people can love and seek truth, goodness, and beauty together. We can pretend that our theological and ethical disagreements are not important for a while but the corrosive effects of such pretense are devastating in the long run. Truth matters. Goodness matters. Beauty matters.

But that presents an enormous problem. What kind of theology and ethics can really work to make sense of pluralism in an intentional Christian community that aims to transcend cultural and ideological polarization? For a church to assert truths of denomination and Bible, doctrine and morals almost always means breaking apart from those who do not possess the truth as that church understands it. Understandably, the moderate church tends to fudge truth questions as a result. After all, if we get too clear about the truth, won't we drive people apart?

There is a way forward here. But the path is not easy. Just as *Lost in the Middle?* requires study in order to win a deep understanding of the situation of the moderate Christian, so *Found in the Middle!* calls for effortful reading. Nothing less will allow us to come to grips with the sort of theology and ethics that can work for individual Christians who love the middle and for the intentional communities that set their lamp on a stand there.

As in the previous book, we will continue to use the familiar "liberal" and "evangelical" labels, hopefully now infused with unfamiliar and wondrous meaning. We can't sidestep these terms without perpetuating the very fudging that we criticize in this book. And we don't want to avoid them because they naturally describe important features of a vibrant faith and a radically inclusive church community.

A SURVEY OF THE TERRITORY

The five parts of this book can guide you on a serious quest for a humble theology, an intelligible gospel message, a compelling view of church unity, and radical ethics that are deeply satisfying to most Christians with both liberal and evangelical instincts. This vision for discerning moderate Christianity self-consciously positions itself between and also above the warring factions of liberal versus evangelical identity politics. We aim to furnish you with tools to help you name and claim your faith in an intellectually robust way.

Part I presents the central theological principle for a liberal-evangelical form of Christianity, the affirmation that God is a vital yet finally incomprehensible reality and cannot be forced to fit human moral and conceptual categories. The Bible consistently conveys not only an invitation to love and serve God, but also a critique of the all-too-human temptation to tame God through social control and theological concepts, which is one source of the sin of idolatry. Faith is especially gripping when we refuse these temptations.

Part II analyzes the central Christological principle for a liberal-evangelical form of moderate Christianity, namely, that God was in Christ reconciling the world. This defines a compelling gospel message of Christ-centered reconciliation while preserving flexibility on the most controversial questions of Christian doctrine that trigger shrill Christian infighting and drive churches apart.

Part III considers the plight of moderate Christian churches from an ecumenical and theological point of view. How do we manage conflicting opinions and fighting in churches? We hail the wisdom of persevering in love despite disagreements. We also acknowledge the inevitability of church splits and so endeavor to avoid an excessively idealistic approach to Christian unity. But we criticize rigid doctrinal purists on both wings for their tendency to embrace church splits as the best way to honor the truth. This approach derives unity and purity from social control rather than from Christian love. Embracing diversity in a liberal-evangelical church causes serious problems for congregational unity, to be sure. But the resulting challenge is precisely what makes Christian unity a vital testimony to the unifying power of Christ in a world that either quickly agrees to disagree or else fights bitterly over the truth with no resolution.

Part IV focuses on practical questions of spirituality, discipleship, and Christian moral priorities. The key principle in this case is Christ-centeredness, articulated in radical discipleship and radical inclusiveness. We explain the meaning of radical Christian discipleship in terms of several factors: the ecclesial call to create Christian community in the face of at least some degree of ideological and theological disagreement, the evangelical call to make disciples in the face of religious diversity, the spiritual call to follow Jesus Christ in the face of a culture sometimes hostile to Christian values, and the intellectual call to embrace a theology that comprehends pluralism and fearlessly asserts the importance of Jesus Christ as a model for spirituality and service. We explain the meaning of radical inclusiveness in terms of the biblical call to follow the bracing example of Jesus's open-hearted and open-armed ministry. This inclusiveness defines the core moral agenda for liberal-evangelical Christians, which subsequently evolves into ethical principles of justice and agape love.

Part V presents a compact guide for liberal-evangelical Christians in the form of seven practical principles for a form of living Christianity that transcends the liberal versus evangelical conflict. This involves partly repenting the conflict, and partly claiming elements of both sides. These principles give local congregations a basis for constructing narratives that sustain congregational unity and mission, even in the face of a certain degree of theological, moral, spiritual, and political disagreement.

We believe that many Christian pastors, seminary students, and lay leaders intuitively sense this moderate yet radical possibility for the Christian movement in our time but feel unsupported and unrepresented in the clamor of contemporary Christianity. We then focus on identifying meaningful "next steps" in parting words specifically for pastors, seminary students, and lay leaders, whom we take to be our constituency and the primary audience for this book.

Acknowledgments

We have enjoyed and profited from the many dozens, surely hundreds, of conversations about one or another aspect of this book in a host of diverse contexts with an unendingly colorful array of fascinating people. As in our previous volume, this book is full of true stories, and only true stories, modified to maintain confidentiality. To readers who might recognize themselves in these stories, we are grateful for the roles they have played in forming our thinking.

Wildman gave several lectures on the radical ethics of Christian moderates, including some material from this book, at the Oikos Scholars Program within Oklahoma City University. Our thanks go to Mark Davies, John Starkey, Dann May, and the enthusiastic audiences at those lectures for their hospitality and helpful feedback.

We are delighted to acknowledge Richard Bass's support of our efforts, beginning with publishing a summary of chapter 13 in the Alban Institute's *Congregations* magazine, and eventually leading to the publication of this book for a wider audience. Our highly skilled editor, Virginia Amos, was a pleasure to work with at every stage of the process.

The website LiberalEvangelical.org aims to empower radically moderate Christians and to offer resources for creatively inclusive congregations. That website contains study guides for this book and for its companion volume, *Lost in the Middle?*, as well as a host of other useful resources. We are pleased to acknowledge the Center for Practical Theology at Boston University School of

Theology for a faculty research grant that helped to support the construction of that site. We are grateful to Dr. Brandon Daniel-Hughes for his skillful proofing and indexing work on this volume and on its companion volume. We are particularly glad to acknowledge his genius as a blogger and reporter, which have helped to make the LiberalEvangelical.org site so valuable for so many Christian moderates.

We are writers formed in "primal communities" of Christians: families, congregations, and seminaries. This is where we have done most of our learning about the frustrations of moderate Christians and their need for an intellectually and emotionally satisfying solution to their profound and instinctive questions about theology and ethics. It is with those primal communities in mind that we dedicate this book to our fathers. The theological and ethical perspective we present in this book may not be the longed-for answer that some moderate Christians seek, but we hope it will be that for many.

PART I

God of the Storm

CHAPTER 1

Approaching God Theologically

A Seminary Journey

Molly and Jane were identical twins, and close like most twins are. They grew up in a Christian home in the Midwest of the United States and eventually claimed their inherited faith with great seriousness. Having been inseparable through high school, they followed different paths in college. One studied biology at a college a couple of hours' drive from the family farm and the other attended an urban university on the West Coast to get a degree in English literature. One married straight out of college and soon had a child, while the other remained happily single and a very proud aunt. Both had jobs in different parts of the country but spoke constantly on the phone and caught up with each other in person as often as they could. Their favorite topic of conversation was the baby but they talked about their faith a lot, too.

In fact, at twenty-five years of age, both Molly and Jane were becoming restless. At a big family gathering one Thanksgiving, with the baby sleeping and everyone else busy, they found time to talk privately. They both felt that they had vastly outgrown the faith support systems of their local communities of faith. The scientist Jane sensed that there was little room in her church community to ask serious questions about how traditional Christian beliefs cohere with the world of nature as modern science discloses it. English major Molly, now an editor working from home while she took care of the baby, was frustrated with the wooden way that her local church community approached the Bible. They wanted to go deeper in faith, and they wanted to do it together. So they hatched a plan. They would go to seminary.

The following autumn, Molly and Jane were back in school, this time on the East Coast, where neither had lived before. Molly's husband was supportive of the move and willingly found a new job. The two parents and the aunt shared responsibility for the precious child in their midst and with a bit of help from a local childcare center they had their lifestyles under control. Most importantly, the twins had energy and time to study and think, to read and write, to pray and talk. They had chosen their seminary carefully. They wanted a place that would support their Christ-centered faith, their profoundly inclusive ethical outlook, and their eagerness to learn from all forms of human knowledge and from all kinds of wisdom traditions. The twins were what we call liberal and evangelical Christians, and like so many moderates, were really quite radical in their faith outlook. So they listened politely to all the well-intended but often parochial warnings about seminary cultures, they gathered information about everything from professors to financial aid, and together they made a clear-headed decision. It was one they would celebrate for the rest of their lives. In fact, a lot of schools would have been able to nurture and transform their faith in the way their chosen school did but they felt they had hit the jackpot and relished every class and every conversation.

When they first arrived in the seminary, they heard a lot of rumors about what was about to happen to them. "Seminary chews you up and spits you out." "Seminary is one long existential crisis." "Seminary makes you question everything you ever believed and makes you believe anything you ever questioned." "Seminary wears you out and leaves you exhausted before it graduates you and then deposits you, with absolutely no convictions left, in the pulpit of a local church, from which position you can give a solid account of the four-source theory of the gospels but you can't actually preach the gospel." The twins never bought into those rumors and quickly diagnosed the purpose they serve. They help students transition from the relative comfort of congregational cocoons to the complex reality of a cosmopolitan seminary. They help entering students bond in the same way that boot camp helps new soldiers become an effective fighting unit.

But the rumors also made the twins angry. They felt the scare tactics demeaned seminary students and distorted the nature of the seminary calling. The rumors make it seem as though students entering seminary were somehow unwilling victims of a devious process designed to frustrate rather than educate, to terrify rather than satisfy, to eviscerate rather than cultivate. But the twins never felt any of that. From their point of view, if their fellow students wanted or needed to think of seminary as a traumatizing, obfuscating waste of time, then they should just leave and find something else to do for a living that felt rewarding and satisfying. The twins were not interested in deceptive, self-protective rumors; they were determined to think and experience for themselves.

Years later, they would recall three powerful experiences from the early weeks of that seminary journey. The first was sitting together in the Hebrew Bible and New Testament classes and sensing an utterly thrilling liberation rising within them as the Bible was unfolded in all of its complicated glory. At last, they were being encouraged to take the Bible seriously without pretending that it was a literal storehouse of divine truths. That was their first moment of deep conviction that they had made the right choice to come to seminary, and to their chosen seminary in particular.

The second memorable experience occurred in the church history class. While both were fairly well educated, the twins really knew nothing about the history of global Christianity, and nothing at all about the formation of the church in the early centuries of its life. They were amazed at the diversity of belief and practice, the violence of the disagreements, and the ways decisions were made and imposed on those who lost the fights. These stories made them deeply thankful for the freedom to believe according to their conscience—a freedom that they had experienced in all of the churches to which they had belonged. Unlike many of their forebears in the faith, they could differ from the standard line without undue fear of punishment or ridicule. They recognized that their approach was more individualistic and frankly more American than was typical of the history of the church, but they were glad about that. On the whole, they felt they were living in a fabulous time and place, where the main problem was taking for granted blessings that had been rare in the history of Christianity.

The third memorable experience occurred in a Christian theology class. The class was introducing the theological debates over the nature of Jesus Christ and the nature of God that triggered the pronouncements of the ecumenical councils of Nicaea (325), Constantinople (381), and Chalcedon (451). The twins could remember reciting the associated creeds in church without any genuine curiosity or deep understanding. But everything was different now. They were not sitting beside one another on this occasion but they both distinctly remember searching out each other's face in amazement on several occasions during the lecture and class discussion that followed. Christians did not disagree just on how to baptize, on the role of women in church leadership, or on how to interpret the Bible's teachings on moral controversies of our own day. Christians also disagreed profoundly on the core ideas of faith: Jesus Christ and God. Some in that class would already have known this because of their undergraduate studies but it took Molly and Jane completely by surprise.

It would not be accurate to say that they were upset by this new revelation about their faith heritage. They were temporarily disturbed, perhaps, but something welcome, an overdue realization, was stirring within them at the same time. Their theology class was confirming what they had so often talked about on the phone or when they met together, namely, that God had to be bigger than human imaginations. And that had to remain true even if God made the divine character known somehow through revelation in history, in nature, in the Bible, and in Jesus Christ. Their oft-stated worries about the apparent conflict between Christian theological claims and the theological claims of other religious traditions immediately faded into the background. The same kinds of theological conflicts were already present within Christianity itself!

A potently transformative idea started to form in their minds that day, and looking at each other across the room they could feel it happening together. Part of the idea was familiar. It was what they had always discussed, except they felt it much more strongly than ever thanks to their accumulating knowledge. God is an all-surpassing reality that exceeds in richness and in sheer intensity of being everything in this world, including the loftiest theological ideas, the highest moral insights, and the most gripping spiritual experiences. The new part of the idea was that this was welcome and wonderful, even as it was strange and terrifying. And it changed everything. Theology was no longer a matter of decoding secret messages to discern the theological truth amidst cultural noise. Now it was a journey of discovery within perpetually uncharted territory, spiritually risky in some ways, and yet the right attitude seemed not to be fear or even deadly earnestness so much as humble joyfulness.

Everything they studied came to life for them after this. Every moment of church history, every struggle between church and culture, every ethical conundrum, every interpretative puzzle in the Bible, every liturgical innovation, and every religious experience was reframed. Instead of being separated phenomena, they were welded together in a vision of tradition-guided questing for home in the divine life. They were utterly convinced that this corporate spiritual journeying in the ambit of divine mystery bound people together more tightly than any shared political ideology or doctrinal consensus. If only the fighting religious factions of this world could see it. For the twins, this was the most transformative insight that human beings could ever have: the all-surpassing ultimate reality was in fact the source of our love for one another, and the wellspring of compassion between all living creatures. We strive and struggle for that kind of orientation, and build bulwarks of doctrine and traditions of practice to "handle" and "tame" the Great Mystery in local groups of like-minded souls. But the truth is bigger than all of us. It can take us to a place where we need less protection from uncertainty than we expected, and where we can love people who are different from us with more intensity than we believed possible.

The twins had fallen in love with God all over again. Only this time their image of God was one they could never outgrow and one that would never lose its wondrous quality.

HUMILITY

The doctrinal orientation of many branches of Christianity produces complicated theories about God and furious disagreements over theological details that—let's be direct about this—most Christians cannot even grasp. The experience of the twins in seminary describes a real possibility for any curious Christian, or indeed any student of any religion. It points to the core theological insight of liberal-evangelical Christianity into divine reality. And it determines the attitudes that such Christians bring to the business of God-talk—an attitude infused with humility.

Humility is essential to theology of all sorts, within and beyond Christianity. But it is the cardinal virtue of liberal-evangelical theology. A liberal-evangelical Christian believes that God was revealed through Jesus Christ, and yet recognizes that the infinite divine reality will always beggar human imaginative and reasoning powers. Speaking of God as revealed in Scripture is essential, and yet any Bible-based God-talk must be tempered by humility because all media in the created world are finite while God is infinite. All our beliefs and descriptions of God are necessarily incomplete and filtered through cognitive structures. As third-world Christians are quick to remind us Westerners, moreover, from their perspective our grandest theological ideas also profoundly reflect our cultural perspectives.

The question of humility echoes through the story of Job and personally challenges each one of us.

> Then the LORD answered Job out of the storm. He said: "Who is this that darkens my counsel with words without knowledge? Brace yourself like a man; I will question you and you shall answer me. Where were you when I laid the foundations?" (Job 38:1–4a NIV)

The answer is simple: we were nowhere to be seen, so we must be humble when we ask to be heard on matters of faith.

Theologians often seem to take their own ideas and words with unlimited seriousness. But the best of them know those deep thoughts are scattered by one puff of the divine breath. Swiss theologian Karl Barth, whose *Church Dogmatics* runs to extremes in length and profundity and sheer mass, knew this. He reportedly pictured himself being cursed to wander the gold-paved streets of heaven forever pulling behind him a trolley loaded up with his books—we picture a child's Red Flyer trolley and a joyful Karl Barth, grateful just to be there, tugging his ridiculous trolley along behind him. Saint Thomas Aquinas knew it, too. He supposedly lapsed into silence near the end of his life after a vision of God convinced him of the utter inadequacy of his theological works, which many since have regarded as definitive for Catholic theology. His majestic writings had become nothing more than a pile of straw to him.

Enthusiastic Christians also seem to take their theological ideas and the theological concepts embedded in their prayers with unlimited seriousness. This is particularly disturbing to the theologian and pastor because such enthusiastic folk often have not bothered to read even something basic that can serve as a guide to Christian theology. It is as if such Christians believe they can reproduce the entire accumulated wisdom of the Christian tradition from their own untutored minds. Or perhaps they believe there is nothing of value in the Christian tradition to be learned and by which to be formed. If it is not simple ignorance, then it is the height of arrogance. Yet Christians with some life experience and maturity in faith know the deeper reality. They have seen gleaming theological ideas shatter on the rocks of experience like a brand new car whose driver is traveling too fast to navigate a mountain curve. They can discern the way human beings use crisp ideas in futile attempts to control divine reality. They know that God surpasses all understanding. In other words, they have become humble.

We are not saying that theology is useless or unimportant. It is inevitable so it should be done as well as possible, and it certainly can be done better and worse. Liberal Christians too often surrender the ideal of standards for theology and implicitly defend the right of every Christian to think and feel and say whatever he or she wants about theological matters. But there is no cause for such defeatism in the face of the genuine theological pluralism of the Christian tradition and the difficulties pluralism presents for attaining well-supported theological beliefs. There is work to be done: theological debates to be charted and relived, creative ideas and new contexts to reckon with, Christians to educate about their own tradition, other religions and philosophies to understand, and truth to be sought in the process. The tools for these tasks are our very best ideas and our sustained devotion to an enormously complex tradition. Theology can become more exciting, and need not lose its appeal, in face of the religious pluralism of our time. The very fact of the pluralism of theological ideas within and beyond the Christian tradition can take us more deeply into the ultimate reality we seek to engage with all our heart and soul and mind and strength.

Against the faint hearts of liberal Christians who give up standards in theology for fear that they are meaningless, we urge less disappointment and an end to despair. The disappointment betrays an optimistic expectation that—surprise, surprise—lacks humility. The faintheartedness hints at hubris that we know in advance what is possible and what is not in theological exploration, so that we can decide from the outset what is worth trying. Greater humility reduces disappointment and produces resolve. The possibilities for theology appear very different when motivation shifts from the desire for perfect understanding and conceptual control over the object of theology to a simple but passionate desire to engage that with which theology has to do—God.

We are not only resisting antitheological liberal Christians, however. Like our liberal-evangelical forbears, we are also launching a broadside attack on the conservative evangelical ideal of doctrinal purity. It is a faithless and foolish fiction that has very little to do with the actual character of God and Christ and salvation and a great deal to do with trying to control other people, often for the sake of securing a corporate identity against the actual pluralism of religious ideas and practices. Conservative evangelicals too often use doctrinal purity as the basis for rules that stipulate who counts and who does not, who is in and who is out, and who is saved and who is damned. Completely forgetting the stunningly inclusive character of Jesus's message of God's reign, they turn the holy gospel into a club with which to beat people, especially other Christians. They exchange Christ's healing touch for the ear-blocked, heart-stopped violence of insecurity that crushes souls and harms the body of Christ.

When it comes to the function of theology within the church, conservative evangelicals are especially sensitive to problems of authority. Sort out where the authority for divine truth comes from and they believe that all uncertainty will be eliminated. For them authority comes from a blend of biblical propositions read through the lens of much later Reformed creedal statements, even though most only speak of biblical inerrancy as if the traditions springing from the Reformation creeds played no role in their interpretative approach to the Bible. There is an authority problem surrounding theology generally and ideas of God in particular. That is why we need an appropriately flexible and multifaceted approach to biblical interpretation. But the very idea of a definitive conceptual picture of God, Jesus Christ, and salvation is thoroughly unbiblical, no matter what authorities we rely on for determining what it would be. No doctrinal statements can possibly comprehend the fierce reality of the God who speaks from the storm and demands to know why we persist in theological chattering. To put absolute trust in any doctrinal portrayal of divine reality is to fall prey to idolatry. Absolute trust should be reserved for absolute reality alone.

The temptation to attach absolute trust to doctrinal formulations is understandable because it derives from our insatiable need for confidence, especially about matters of ultimate importance to us. But the mature Christian, like the seasoned theologian, learns to discern the spiritual danger lurking beneath the surface of such passionate motivations. Theological understanding of the contents of faith cannot be captured in a doctrinal jar like a firefly after which we can behold its beauty with wonder and awe. For Christians, theological understanding is a lifelong journey during which our souls are slowly forged under the impress of the image of Christ. Our quest for understanding is answered not by neat doctrinal statements or bumper-sticker slogans but by being informed by Christ within the communities and traditions that his life and ministry breathed into being.

CHAPTER 2

God Talk

Sizing Up God

One of our liberal-evangelical heroes, J. B. Phillips, once wrote a book with a title that we love: *Your God Is Too Small.* Phillips's message was right on target, for his context and also for ours. It doesn't matter how smart you are, how good you are, or how attractive you are. It doesn't matter how much you read the Bible, how much you pray, or how much you give to church and charity. It doesn't matter what your culture is, what your gender is, what your skin color is. It doesn't matter who your relatives are or who you know, where you went to school or where you live. Your God is too small.

Like many difficult truths, the people who cannot easily accept this fact of human life are also the people who need to hear it most urgently. Some people make God so small that God actually vanishes from their lives. These people assume that, since it seems unlikely anything conclusive could ever be known about God, if God even exists, it is best not to bother trying to get to know God at all. In Christian circles, it is more common to encounter people making God too small through believing that they fully understand God and God's motives. They create or absorb an image of God that is probably related to the Bible and reflective of their local community's culture of Christian belief. But then they allow this image to take the place of the actual God, relating to the image exclusively rather than using the image to relate to a God who breaks all images. Worst of all, they often speak proudly about who God is and what God wants, as if they were the one speaking from the eye of the storm. And they sometimes speak in a way that is desperately limited by superficial understanding of the Bible and very limited self-awareness.

The Bible contains ample resources to disrupt prideful ignorance and launch immature Christians into the deeper waters of faith. The Bible's striking images of God collectively express a persistent refusal of the conceit that God can be captured in a consistent set of human concepts. They also affirm the spiritual practice of imaginatively engaging God through diverse images, sometimes heartwarming and sometimes disturbing.

God is likened to various parts of nature such as darkness-excluding light, thirst-quenching water, a rock, a mountain, a breeze, a whirlwind, a cloud, and a pillar of fire. God is likened to animals such as a hen, an eagle, a brooding bird, a moth, a bear, a wild ox, a lion, a leopard, and a lamb. God is pictured as a tower, a shield, and a garment. God is described using social roles and activities such as creator, potter, refiner, architect, covenanter, advocate, lawyer, legislator, law-giver, lord, king, warrior, judge, executioner, avenger, destroyer, redeemer, shepherd, protector, provider, physician, business owner, farmer, father, birthing mother, nursemaid, disciplinarian, husband, cuckold, and bridegroom. God is assigned human qualities and responses such as intelligence, will, memory, anger, fury, disappointment, sadness, grief, revenge, promise-making, forgiveness, love, passion, and planning. God is spoken of as possessing human form, with eyes, arms, hands, feet, a face, a mouth, and a back; and also as walking around, speaking with a voice, smelling, and having an appearance.

The Christian spiritual and theological traditions are also filled with stunning images of God. Many of these images have biblical roots but they are borne up on other wings: the dual facts of experiencing the incomprehensibility of divine reality on the one side and experiencing the possibility of authentic engagement with God through images on the other side. This vast treasure chest of images is stocked especially with ideas that spring from the liturgical and mystical domains of religious experience. Here we mention just one as an example of the wealth of images sustained within the Christian tradition: God as darkness. The Bible so often pictures God as light that the mystical image of

God as darkness can seem strange at first. But this provocative image describes the encounter with something that surpasses understanding, which we experience especially through the inadequacy of all concrete images.

There is even a spiritual practice within mysticism known as the *via negativa* (the way of negating) in which every name and attribute of God is denied out of faithfulness to God's image-transcending nature. This meditative process can propel the mind into a kind of conceptual darkness in which God is engaged less through concrete images and more through releasing our hold on all images. This is a luminous and joyous darkness, in one way, but it can also be emotionally oppressive and even terrifying. The glory of God is dangerous to human beings, as the Bible so often describes, and the terror of God's holiness is not controlled or canceled by God's love. C. S. Lewis realized this when he used a frightening yet loving lion as an image of the divine presence in his *Chronicles of Narnia*. In the same way, darkness and light tumble together in mystical imagery, reflecting the complementary aspects of relationship with God.

Popular culture also uses images to engage our imagination as we reflect on God, especially through contemporary movies and literature. Some of these images are supportive of widespread religious responses, as when God is pictured as a wise old man (George Burns in *Oh God* or Morgan Freeman in *Bruce Almighty* and *Evan Almighty*). Other images of God seem calculated to provoke a response of surprise or puzzlement in watchers and readers, or to highlight an aspect of God's nature that the filmmaker or author believes usually goes unnoticed. So God is pictured as an attractive woman (Jessica Lange as Angelique, a personification of Death) in *All that Jazz*. In the controversial comic farce *Dogma,* which attacks organized religion while affirming faith in God, God is represented both as a frail old man who loves ski-ball and as a wordless young woman (Alanis Morissette) who does playful handstands in the garden and destroys with her roaring voice. Films and literature usually portray God much more indirectly, through the thoughts and feelings of the main characters with whom we identify. In films such as *The Last Temptation of Christ* or *The Passion of Christ*, we picture God indirectly through searing portrayals of the God-man Jesus. Directly and indirectly, these media can effectively explore the contours of religious belief and both confirm and challenge our existing convictions about God.

There is an important difference between rigid attachment to particular God images and the changing psychological realities of the developing human life. When we are young we need concrete images of God to make the divine reality tangible; that is quite appropriate. Throughout our lives we rely on images to articulate and nurture our relationship with God. Such limitations are not a problem in themselves. Picturing God in such a way that we can relate to God is what makes religious life important. God is a loving father or mother, in that we believe we can trust ourselves to God completely. God is a friend or confidant in that we believe God knows our thoughts and needs before we utter them, and it is safe to share our deepest longings with God in prayer. God is judge and avenger, in that we believe that the sin and injustice of the world will encounter a divine reckoning. Our working images of God are tailored to our particular needs for God and to our creative, yet limited, ability to imagine that which we believe but cannot fully conceive. Thus, it is developmentally appropriate and psychologically intelligible to use God images to engage the incomprehensible and image-breaking divine reality.

The problem arises when we begin to think that our favorite image of God is the only one or the best one. We lose track of the contrast between God's infinity and our finite humanity. This tendency may be part of the human condition but it is a trap that mature Christians in every generation learn to avoid. Unfortunately, the history of Christianity is filled with examples of people, sometimes very influential people, who have not reached this level of maturity. Liberals, evangelicals, conservatives, biblical literalists, fundamentalists—all of us—tend to assume we have the inside track in a race to understand God. The Jehovah's Witnesses are certain they are right. The Southern Baptist Convention believes it has the truth well in hand. Bishop Spong knows he is right. The Jesus Seminar thinks it is right. David Koresh believed he was right.

It is a common failing of liberals to feel so socially and educationally superior that any conservative who derives their faith principally from some external authority must be a simpleton who refuses to accept reality. Likewise, conservative evangelicals commonly regard those who disagree with their favorite image of God as spiritually defective and morally impure. We all run the risk of reducing God to a size that fits comfortably into our small lives.

Liberal-evangelical theology combines humility and passion. We believe in God, and we also believe there is more to God than we could ever know. We follow Christ trusting that discipleship helps us by grace to craft lives that are pleasing to the God who is both known and unknown to us, and in fact is known partly *as* unknown. Our images of God are not the same as the reality that the images help us to engage. Liberal evangelicals speak passionately and openly about God, all the while *actively listening and watching* for how the God who surpasses all understanding does not fit our precious ideas. Liberal evangelicals treasure their God images, but they also know their images of God are too small, and they believe that God is big enough to forgive all limitations.

It is important to acknowledge that we often hurt others with our small images of God. Christians have often pictured God as a man, which has reinforced sexual stereotypes and greatly retarded cultural recognition of the true equality of spiritual dignity between men and women. In fact, Christian churches needed to be rescued from this great sin by a secular liberation movement—clear evidence for Christians that the Holy Spirit works outside as well as within the churches. Similarly, white Christians have typically pictured God as white, which helped them rationalize their enslavement of black Africans. Slavery was often seen as a divinely mandated elevation of the supposedly "subhuman" estate of native Africans. It is impossible to believe that white Christians could have reasoned this way had they pictured God as black.

The fact that our small images of God are so socially potent is one of the sources of great evil in the history of human civilization. It is one of the reasons why idolatry is not merely a matter of poor judgment or spiritual immaturity or theological insecurity. A lot can ride on culturally embedded idolatrous God-images. Liberal-evangelical Christianity is primed by its humble expectation that God surpasses all images to be alert to the terrible side-effects of idolatrous attachment to images of God.

THEOLOGICAL CONFLICT

If we accept humility as the watchword for Christian theology, how are we to understand theological disagreement and conflict? Once we realize that we engage God through a wide variety of symbols and images, what is the basis for discerning better and worse ideas of God? On this question, we use ourselves as an illustration.

Garner resonates most with the biblical pictures of God as a divine person, with plans and feelings, aware of each of us in the intimate way that we are aware of our children, and possessing the ability and desire to act in the world of nature and history to express the divine will and to respond to prayers. This personal God is enormously appealing because we understand the image so readily. It can be a source of strength and encouragement in everyday struggles. Sensing that we are being watched over is both comforting and alarming, inducing both trust in God's mercy and a strong attempt to act in such a way that we need not be ashamed in the divine presence. Believing that God hears and answers prayers adds great excitement to daily life. Imagining that God has a unique plan for each of us makes us eager to find out what it is and live into it.

Wildman resonates more with the creedal images of God as an eternal, unchanging principle of power and creativity, beyond the flow of time, and far beyond the human business of feeling and planning, intending and responding. Divine providence is not a matter of answering a prayer but rather of God creating a world with the possibility for humans to build just societies and heal diseases. Divine love is not a matter of God experiencing feelings of compassion and care but rather of God creating a world that supports human civilization and adventure and nurtures the possibility of love and care. This God is more transcendent than the personal God and also more intensely immanent through being intimately present in and through the very patterns of nature that define human life, the very physical processes that support our embodied way of being. As Muslims like to say, in a striking image, God is closer than our jugular vein.

Interestingly, though we (Garner and Wildman) *understand* both ideas of God, they are not equally *appealing* to us. On the one hand, to Garner, who is used to thinking of God as a personal being, the idea of God as a creative principle, as *being itself* (as Saint Augustine and Saint Thomas liked to say), seems cold and impersonal, offering little sense of purpose for life and slim hope for the future. It seems morally disastrous because there is no divine personality whose intimate knowledge of our lives ramifies our experiences of pain and suffering, and no divine architect able to devise—and willing to implement—a plan to fix the mess human beings have made for themselves.

On the other hand, to Wildman, who prefers thinking of God in terms of the ancient theological categories (immutability, impassibility, infinity, eternity), the personal idea of God seems unbelievably anthropomorphic, a kind of fairy-tale version of the real thing. It also seems morally disastrous since it leaves us asking why God does not act to alleviate needless suffering and cruelty just as a loving parent surely would act to protect his or her children from harm caused by their own stupidity or the aggression of others.

Each of us understands the other's point of view but honestly feels that one of the two sets of coordinated God images (we might call them God theories) is more truthful, and better for engaging God in everyday life. We explain how this difference arises in terms of varying personality types, intellectual styles, and histories of personal development. In fact, these two contrasting God theories have deep roots in the Christian theological tradition. Christian theologians have typically tried to combine them so as to honor both sides of the tradition but the syntheses have never been truly coherent, even in their most influential forms, such as the theologies of Augustine and Aquinas just mentioned.

There is something incommensurable in the personal and principle types of God theories. Any combination of them in a theological system loses balance and falls more toward one side or the other, or else holds the two sides in an unresolved tension. The two of us illustrate the way this occurs. In search of a coherent God theory, each of us does fall more to one side than the other. But in honor of traditional Christian wisdom and biblical wisdom, we respect those who fall the other way, as well as those who try to hold the two sides together even though the result does not quite make sense. We respect these approaches different from our own because we understand that God is ultimately beyond our conceptual grasp, and because what we *can* understand—the history of ideas of God—strikes us wonderful in its diversity.

Theological Debate Ruled by Humility and Love

With this concrete example in place—and to us it is a very personal illustration—we can restate our question. How can there be meaningful theological debate between us both, and thus between these two theological theories of God? If we can't appeal to some outside authority to settle the question of which God idea is more adequate, how can we avoid the disaster of an anything-goes theology, after which the very idea of standards for theological reflection collapses? And if we do appeal to an outside authority to settle the debate, how do we avoid falling prey to self-serving arbitrariness? Do we use the Bible's more personal idea of God to attack the more philosophical idea? Do we use the philosophical categories from the early creedal history of Christianity to supplement and interpret the personalist outlook of the biblical witness? Do we listen to whatever the pope says or to what our local pastor says and just believe that? We present a way of thinking about theological debate that is ruled by humility and love, in four stages.

First, *we honor the Bible by remembering core-message pluralism* (we discussed this at length in *Lost in the Middle?*). Liberal-evangelical Christians do look to the Bible, but not as a definitive source of doctrinal propositions against which we can sort through the history of theology and creeds, tossing out some God ideas because they do not measure up and affirming others because they do. Properly acknowledging core-message pluralism makes that impossible; the core message of Christianity was *always* diverse, from the beginning until now. Rather, the Bible is the source for classic God images that nurture the entire tradition of Christian theology and spirituality. For both of us, the Bible's authority is more *causal* (what it does) than *propositional* (how it theorizes). The Bible's deepest effect is helping us to understand that God surpasses human comprehension. This means that the Bible itself stands in the way of too decisive a resolution of questions of theology—that's what it *does*. So it would be a mistake by biblical standards for either of us to conclude that our favored God theory was perfectly correct and the other plain wrong. We would be foolish to suppose that our favored God idea can serve as the ultimate standard for theological debate. Our best ideas don't define theological truth and they don't justify the exclusion of alternative God ideas and the people who hold them. In other words, we take core-message pluralism seriously and do not rush to oversimplify the complexity of theological ideas.

Second, *we love and learn the Christian tradition.* Liberal-evangelical Christians also look to tradition, but not as a definitive source of wisdom that settles all theological debates. Instead, we ponder its debates and treasure them as the earlier versions of some of the fights we have in our own day. We teach the conflicted tradition to our children and to adult Christians, not as a rigid barrier to creative exploration but as the ultimate source of permission to think for ourselves about divine reality under the guidance of a complex heritage. In this way, we have both discovered that our theological debate about the nature of divine reality resonates backwards and forwards through the Christian tradition, as well as beyond it into the theological and philosophical traditions of other religions. We understand that we had better know something about our heritage if we are to avoid making naive mistakes in our theological reasoning. Yet, we are inspired by that complex tradition to explore our ideas and make them as intellectually compelling and experientially adequate as possible.

Third, *taking God seriously makes a place for determined inquiry.*
Liberal-evangelical Christians, such as the two of us, take the
calling to love God with all our heart and soul and mind and
strength with great seriousness. This means that we must explore
our theological ideas rather than just take them for granted. We
are free to think and inquire, not just accept and believe. It also
means we must learn that what seems convincing to us could easily transform several times as faith perpetually deepens through
the course of a lifetime. So we both had better get to know the
strengths and weaknesses of our favored ideas of God. We had
better learn how to argue for one over the other, and hopefully
even get good at defending the view we find less appealing as
a test of our understanding of the debate. We had better argue
with each other—courteously but with determination borne of
the experience of engaging God through our favorite imagistic
theories of divine reality. We can treasure such moments of re-
spectful argument as joyous and good-hearted explorations of
that which fascinates us ultimately.

Determined inquiry is not everyone's cup of tea, to be sure.
Therefore, people not suited to it might feel uncomfortable with
it, but they should not try to prevent others from doing it. And
those who are suited to theological inquiry should not forget
that we debate theories of that which ultimately passes human
understanding. Conclusions about what is better and worse in
theological theories of God must be perpetually provisional
judgments. But the judgments can still be made and reasoned
opinions can still be held and justified. For example, a lot of in-
ferior concepts of God are passed by on the way to the personal
and principle theories that have such a prominent place within
the Christian tradition (and indeed other theistic traditions as
well). While those two heavyweights have not been able to knock
each other out of the competition of ideas, the two certainly have
knocked out other ideas that have not competed well in terms
of conceptual power or consistency and coherence. All of these
results of theological inquiry are encoded in the history of Christian thought—another reason to know that history.

Fourth, *theological debate is a marathon, not a sprint.* Liberal-
evangelical Christians put all of this together in a life-long jour-

ney of humility and love. Wildman is fairly sure that Garner's idea of God is deficient. He has learned the Christian tradition's ways of struggling with these competing intuitions about divine reality so he knows both how to make the strongest case on behalf of his own view and what its greatest theoretical weaknesses and spiritual dangers are. He accepts that he has to take his own view seriously enough to argue with Garner's opposed view. But Wildman also remembers how he grew into his view, and how others like him have changed their viewpoints. He knows that God surpasses comprehensive understanding so his theological theory of God retains the quality of an existential bet, no matter how well he argues for it. Thus he feels joy in the debate and freedom in making his theological bet, picturing this as a kind of trusting theological play in the divine sandbox, over which God (to use personal imagery) would smile in the same way we smile at the childlike determination of our own children at play. Most importantly, Wildman loves his opponent, treats him with respect, and works with him on shared projects. *And what is true of Wildman is also true of Garner, point for point.* The liberal-evangelical ideal of theological debate demands rigorous argument but also stresses love of opponents and humility before the God whose nature is unendingly fascinating and inspiring. And we take care not to cause others to stumble because of our theological debates.

This way of understanding how theological debate works supports intricate theological inquiry, painstaking historical analysis of theological tradition, and creative interaction with other areas of human knowledge and other heritages of theological and philosophical wisdom. It will never satisfy many conservative evangelicals and fundamentalists because it does not tie down all the loose ends, and that invites a problem with authority and Christian identity. Nor will it satisfy many liberals because they just can't see the point of theological debate if we have any reason in advance to suspect that definitive resolution is not possible. But that marks out what is theologically distinctive about liberal-evangelical Christians. The distinctiveness lies not in doctrine but in an approach of radical discipleship that is faithful to the comprehension-surpassing character of divine reality.

Conservative evangelicals are right in that this liberal-evangelical approach to theological debate does invite authority and identity problems. But moderates have always lived with those problems, and they intuitively recognize that such problems are unavoidable in life, so there is nothing new here for them. The liberals are right that (1) intense and rigorous theological debate seems to stand in direct tension with (2) properly acknowledging theological diversity and the comprehension-defying nature of divine reality. To the liberal-evangelical Christian, however, these two are *mutually reinforcing practices* and both rise in strength together. Theirs is not a survival-minded or confidence-oriented or identity-obsessed approach to theological discussion. It is not an easy way and it will never be wildly popular, given the social and psychological realities of religious individuals and groups, but it is deep and true and simple.

We take theological debate seriously because we love the God we fight about. We take loving our theological opponents seriously because living in love is more important than theological play. And we take the provisional character of our God theories seriously because we must be humble before the God who passes all understanding.

THE QUALITY OF GOD-TALK

Liberal evangelicals are likely to steer away from long catalogues of divine attributes and vast webs of logically ordered propositions about God's nature. By contrast, this sort of intricacy is a favorite approach of conservative evangelical theologians, especially if they are Reformed in heritage. Catholics have their own version of this approach in some traditions of theological thought and Christian education. Christians know less about such matters than these intellectual endeavors suggest, however, and liberal evangelicals typically prefer theology to remain consistent with that fact of life. If liberal evangelicals say anything at all about divine reality, therefore, it will have five characteristics:

- It will be simple and direct.
- It will not stray far from our experience.
- It will take account of the pluralism of Christian theological resources for speaking of God.
- It will take full responsibility for interpreting divine self-revelation in Scripture and tradition.
- It will remember its own provisional status. We say a word about each of these five characteristics in what follows.

First, the simple and direct approach follows the example of most Christian creeds over the centuries. There was significant wisdom present in the church councils that produced those creeds. Partly because of the political pressures in each context, they usually forged statements of Christian belief with a close to optimal degree of detail. To use an analogy with television, super-high definition creeds are not appropriate for Christians who think of God as surpassing all comprehension. And a badly fuzzy creedal picture is just irritating and conveys nothing useful for theology or Christian identity. The best creeds use clear reception but low resolution.

Second, resolving not to stray far from our experience is a hedge against runaway speculation in God-talk. Some human beings love speculative stories and extrapolating exquisitely detailed doctrinal systems from mere hints. But theology at its most useful is second-order reflection on first-order experiences of life, including Christian worship and service. We can appreciate speculation, of course, but we must not allow it to cut theology off from its practical experiential grounding. We must be especially wary of the social controllers who would impose those speculations on everyone, as requirements for faith. Christian faith is worthy of the most energetic rational reflection and the most careful study, but first and foremost it is an experience of salvation and a lifestyle of discipleship.

Third, liberal evangelicals recognize that there is a great pluralism of Christian theological resources for speaking of God. This is a gift because it reminds us that authentic theological reflection on Christian experience can take us in many directions.

It is virtually impossible to hold a viewpoint that has not been both asserted and challenged multiple times within the Christian tradition. The first-order experiences of Christian life are not scripts to be read directly into theology but are rather more like jewels whose facets sparkle into manifold visions of beauty. This is confusing, to be sure, and some people would prefer to pick one facet and ignore the rest. But liberal-evangelical Christians typically feel suspicious around over-crisp or narrow doctrinal formulations because they instinctively sense that the divine reality cannot be condensed into a convenient form for needy religious consumers. They would rather appreciate the whole diamond, not just a facet of it.

Fourth, precisely because God is fundamentally beyond human control and comprehension, human God-talk always presupposes divine self-revelation. Divine reality is available for experience, rational understanding, and theological reflection, yes, but never so neatly that its multifaceted jewel-like character is abrogated. Indeed, the manifold traditional resources for God-talk faithfully portray the boundary-breaking quality of God's own nature. When we interpret divine self-revelation in Scripture and tradition, therefore, it is a human creative response to divine revelation, and we must take full responsibility for our part in that interaction. We must not get muddled about the infinitely important distinction between divine revelation and our reception of it. To pretend that our God-talk is a matter of logical inference from propositional revelation in the Bible or in sacred tradition is to posture at controlling divine reality. It is futile to try to tame God in this way, but it is also dangerous because we can do great harm to ourselves and others.

Fifth and finally, all of our God-talk has provisional status because it is our creation, not God's. It is rooted in the complicated swirl of human experience and multifaceted traditions of interpretative wisdom, not plucked from the sky. For the liberal-evangelical Christian, assurance of faith does not mean certainty about the truth of Christian doctrinal statements. Rather, it means that we authentically engage God through our creedal exertions, through our worship and service, through our lives of love, and even through our God-talk.

CHAPTER 3

In the Grip of a God Beyond Our Grasp

God is *ultimately* beyond human concepts, but not so *utterly* beyond them that we cannot engage God authentically through theological reflection. This is to draw a distinction between quantity and quality: divine reality is qualitatively beyond cognitive grasp but, quantitatively speaking, God is everywhere encountered and engaged in the worlds of nature and experience. When Saint Augustine faced the paradox of speaking about the unspeakable, he immediately recognized the fundamental reason to speak: how can we remain silent about that which so captivates us, about that which is of ultimate concern to us? So we speak. And we get into trouble. And we fix our mistakes. And we continue in a perpetual paradox of talking about a God ultimately (quality!) but not utterly (quantity!) beyond our concepts. How should liberal-evangelical Christians manage this paradox?

Keeping in mind the five characteristics of God-talk introduced at the end of the previous chapter, we suggest that statements about God be referred not only to the Bible and sacred tradition but also to concrete aspects of our experience. We experience the world, and so we speak of God as the *whence of the world* (the "from where of the world"); God is creator and sustainer of all reality. We live out our own complex experience in the world, and so we speak of God as the *whence of human existence*; God is the ground of being and our ultimate concern. We experience reconciliation through Christ, and so we speak of God as the *whence of reconciliation*; God is redeemer and savior and transformer. This refer-theology-to-experience approach makes it possible to construct evangelically compelling theological affirmations that come to terms with the pluralism that liberal Christianity correctly recognizes in the Christian tradition, and with the ultimately all-surpassing quality of divine reality.

Thinking of God humbly as the whence of the world, the whence of existence, and the whence of reconciliation—and in this way referring theological reflection to our experience—has theological and doctrinal consequences. These consequences are contestable. Just as the Buddhist story of enlightenment is plausible to millions but to few Christians, so the Christian story of reconciliation is plausible to millions but to few Buddhists. These faith stances and their doctrinal consequences are something like the vast wagers of entire traditions, including the religious communities and people that constitute those traditions. We can recognize that the plausibility of our beliefs depends on those longstanding traditions and the stories they tell, and we can tolerate the uncertainties that result from being aware that our tradition is not the only compelling one, because we cleave to Christ in faith. This is not a dogmatic cleaving that demands naming the Other as evil or deluded. It is cleaving out of love, as a natural response to the experience of reconciliation, just as we cleave to our own families in a special way even though we know there are other wonderful families in the world. It is open, not closed; it is curious, not defensive; and it is confident, not arrogant. For us, this perfectly expresses the liberal-evangelical posture toward the doctrines of Christian creeds and theology.

German theologian Wolfhart Pannenberg and American theologian John Cobb are both well known for their description of the Christian tradition as hypothetical, a kind of vast bet on the future, and understanding this as part of the meaning of faith. Post-liberal theologians of various stripes, including George Lindbeck, are open about doctrine being the grammar of a community of faith, an expression of the way Christians speak and act in the world. All such views explicitly acknowledge that Christian beliefs are plausible when set within particular traditions of literature and art, theology and liturgy, reflection and action. We think this is a properly humble approach to doctrinal elaboration of the basic experiences of being Christian. We love its nondefensiveness and its commitment to tradition. We especially appreciate its sponsorship of an ideal of evangelism as transformative dialogue and mutual encounter. It is with this perspective on Christian doctrine in mind that we devote this chapter to brief discussions of four theological topics that have been more or less definitive for Christian faith.

THE STRANGE NEW WORLD OF THE BIBLE

On Election Day 2004, Leo entered the church that supports his AA group. It is a liberal and evangelical church that hosts numerous twelve-step groups as part of the church's mission to offer an unconditional welcome to God's people. Before Leo entered his meeting, he dropped by the church offices. In a loud and unflinchingly confident voice Leo asked, "Have you all voted today?" And then he said, "I voted like a good Christian for George Bush. In good conscience I had to vote for him."

This raised the ire of most of the church staff who were within earshot, perhaps because they voted differently or perhaps because they did not like politics talked about in public or in such terms. One of the clergy present engaged Leo by sharing carefully and thoughtfully that her Christian conscience had led her to make an alternative choice. "Sure, but as a Christian, you don't believe in all that support of gay marriage stuff? Not as a Christian! Not as a pastor!" Leo continued.

Again the pastor gently offered another take on the issue, which she stated was supported by the church's radically inclusive mission statement. "Well, the Bible is clear: homosexuality is an abomination," Leo boldly asserted.

The pastor then masterfully explained that everyone who reads the Bible does something called "interpretation." "Not me," Leo bellowed. "The Bible is written in black and white, and I only read the black part. I don't understand people who try to read between the lines. I do as the Bible says. That's why I voted for George Bush. If John Kerry wins we are going to have gay people kissing on every street corner in our country. That would be immoral—an abomination—just like it says in the Bible."

The conversation ended with the pastor carefully restating their difference of opinion, and then thanking Leo for the conversation and wishing him God's blessing.

Everyone who picks up the Bible interprets it. The Bible is an ancient text written to ancient people in a culture we can only begin to imagine. We cannot read a text written in the Mediterranean world in the millennium prior to the first century CE and expect it to apply directly to the lives of men and women in the United States of America in the twenty-first century. If we deny the fact of interpretation, or the need to do it well, we quickly run into trouble.

In his correspondence to the Corinthian community, the apostle Paul addressed the community's concerns about food that had been sacrificed to idols (1 Corinthians 8). We simply cannot apply this text directly to our daily life. The pastor who tries to preach the sermon "The Benefits and Liabilities of Eating Meat Sacrificed to Idols" will utterly befuddle the people in his or her congregation. We do not have a "sacrificial meat offering" option in the deli sections of our grocery stores. People who truly believe that Scripture is to be taken literally will have to disregard this passage as irrelevant until live animal sacrifice comes into fashion again. However, if we believe that there is profit in all scripture (2 Tim. 3:14–17), then we need to interpret Scripture in ways that make it relevant to contemporary life. In 1 Corinthians 8, Paul is talking about being careful of our behavior and habits so that we don't function as a stumbling block to weaker believers. Paul's reference to meat sacrifice in the first century could easily be interpreted as drinking, smoking, or office flirtation today. None of those behaviors or habits are sinful in and of themselves, for most Christians, but they can become an issue of real concern if we harm others or cause another person of faith to stumble into spiritually harmful behavior.

Of course, any discerning high-school student can sense the tension that exists between the childhood belief that the Bible and its stories are true, and the reality that the Bible is not an investigative reporter's clear-eyed account of the ancient Hebrew people, with high accuracy, carefully checked facts, and perfect impartiality. Any person thinking critically has to grapple with the juxtaposition of biblical truth and historical uncertainty. Confirmation classes around the world echo with the same adolescent faith questions. "How can anyone stay alive in the belly of a whale for three days?" "How can trumpets topple city walls?" "If the sun stood still that means the earth stopped rotating—that can't happen without total disaster all over the planet." "Why are there two different creation stories?" "If Jesus says he is the only way, what happens to all the people of different faiths in the world?" "How can we know that our faith is right?" Each of these questions can lead to the mistaken assumption that the Bible is just another book that contains some creative stories and tidbits of wisdom.

Moderate Christians with liberal and evangelical instincts take the Bible seriously as a source of authority and grace. While the Bible may not always be historically or scientifically accurate, it contains within its pages the truth and spirit of God. When applied to our lives, the Bible can indeed separate bone from marrow, and flesh from spirit (Heb. 4:12). Careful, thoughtful, and faithful biblical interpretation can rescue the biblical text both from those who take it too literally, and from those who don't take it seriously. Conservative Christians often try to control the meaning of Scripture, while liberal Christians let their Bibles gather dust. Moderate Christians with both liberal and evangelical instincts read their Bibles expecting to encounter the Word of God, believing that the Holy Spirit helps us interpret that ancient Word to transform our twenty-first-century lives. Like Job we can speak of God, speak to God, and speak for God, but in the end we know that we were nothing when God was forming the world, and we will be dust long before God is done with creation. Biblical interpretation requires spiritual humility.

THE HOLY SPIRIT AND THE TRINITY

Being born again is typically one of the most potent events in the lives of those who have experienced it—and something very much like it seems to occur in all religions. When this born-again event is experienced in a Christian way, Jesus Christ's life, death, and resurrection become the touchstones for explaining it. The logic of the explanation is not watertight, and need not be. What matters is the persuasiveness of the explanatory narrative that we tell within the community of believers. Doctrine grows atop these primal experiences and these original acts of narrating them to one another. Doctrinal theology is a secondary process, a reflective synthesis that makes the narrative explanations coherent and consistent. The Bible preserves some of the early layers of explanatory narratives and doctrinal reflections within the Christian movement. Subsequent theological debate and key church councils took things further. Before long there was a vast and intricate assemblage of doctrinal machinery, a lot of which doesn't make sense to ordinary Christians.

The classic example of this is the doctrine of the Trinity. Few Christians even know how to state the Trinitarian doctrine without falling into one (or several) of the heretical formulations that church councils, in their wisdom, sought to rule out. That's a measure of how complicated talking about the all-surpassing divine reality had become by the fifth century. But surely ordinary Christians today can hope for a way to translate the fundamental narrative logic that led the early Christians to such a complex picture of God. Indeed, there is such a way, and it refers doctrine to experience. Here it is.

We presume Jesus Christ died a sacrificial death because that makes sense of our experience of transformation from guilt to gratitude—that can't happen without a price being paid. We believe Jesus Christ is divine because our guilt and despair is such that we are certain we can't get ourselves out of the mess we are in; only God could do it. We assert that Jesus Christ rose from the dead because we encounter the risen Christ as our Savior and Lord in daily life. We know the Holy Spirit is real because it is the practical presence of God in our lives, inspiring us, comforting us, and correcting us. God, as a result of these primal experiences, must be somehow internally related, somehow three in one. In essence, this is why and how the doctrine of the Trinity was born.

It is not difficult to imagine Christians saying, "Hold on a minute; let's not rush ahead of ourselves here. The Holy Spirit is God's presence with us, and it does not need to be a separate person. Jesus Christ may be divine but that would have to be in a metaphorical sense because at a literal level it actually makes no sense. God is One and Christ is God's Messiah, the anointed one whom God makes Lord over all the Earth, just as Peter preached, as recorded in Acts 2." This approach to theologically interpreting the primal Christian experiences of reconciliation has strong biblical credentials, and it has been persuasive to many Christians, all the way up to today. Indeed, Unitarian Christians (not Universalists) made this approach definitive for their denomination, and this view is held privately by many Christians in diverse churches all over the world.

Yet the Christian doctrinal tradition went another way, possibly to put more distance between its own beliefs about Jesus Christ and the obviously Jewish approach of "God is One" and "We still await the Messiah." Christian thinkers explained the apparent contradiction of saying that a finite being (Jesus) is divine by means of a special doctrine called the hypostatic union, which is the key to the coherence of the incarnation narrative. They then explained the internal relations within God using the doctrine of the Trinity, drawing on the machinery of Greek metaphysics. Together, this is what inspired the great doctrinal pronouncements of the Church Councils of Nicea (325), Constantinople (381), and Chalcedon (451).

The practical ramifications of the hypostatic union and the Trinitarian doctrine are mind-boggling. On the one hand, they inspire a vast heritage of art and literature and architecture. On the other hand, they have potent implications for the interpretation of human beings. These implications are worked out most fully in the doctrine of theosis, which posits the idea that God became human in Christ so that human beings could become divine. But even Protestants, who typically reject theosis, portray a connection between God and human beings that is almost unbelievably intimate. Swiss theologian Karl Barth tried to express this in a famous address that he gave late in his life, shockingly entitled "The Humanity of God."

The doctrine of the Trinity, with the hypostatic union, set loose in Western civilization an idea of enormous power whose influence is virtually imponderable. This theoretical duo defines the tradition that flows down to Christians today. It is a complex tradition, internally contested and elaborated in ways that do not win universal acceptance. But it defines a conceptual world for the Christian narratives that explain the primal experiences of reconciliation—a world within which these narratives become deeply plausible and enormously attractive. And that is the sense in which these doctrines are fundamentally rational, the sense in which they are true and good and beautiful. They really can make sense of our experience of reconciliation, once we learn what they mean and how to interpret our experience through the lens that they offer. But we must also remember that God surpasses the conceptual reach of all theologians and all theological theories, even those officially approved in ancient ecumenical councils of church leaders.

MEANING AND PURPOSE OF LIFE, EXISTENCE, AND HISTORY

Christians are led to theological reflection by the deepest and most universal questions that human beings can ask. What is life all about? Why are we here? What is at the heart of this human drama? What is the purpose of creation? Again, the humility of one who was *not there at the beginning* is required when asking such ultimate questions. Within Christianity, once we acknowledge God as the whence of the world, the whence of existence, and the whence of reconciliation, a fairly clear narrative emerges that answers these ultimate questions about the meaning and purpose of life.

As the story of Adam and Eve beautifully and poetically suggests, God desired relationship. The life of a divine spirit hovering over a formless and empty void (Gen. 1:1–2) was apparently less than fully satisfying, so God decided to create. Through that creating, relationship was born—relationships with nature, with the creatures of the natural world, and with human beings. The pain and anguish and disappointment of relationship were born, as well. One of the first truly heartbreaking verses in the Bible follows Adam and Eve's eating from the Tree of Knowledge of Good and Evil. God comes calling, and Adam and Eve are hiding. "Then the man and his wife heard the sound of the Lord God as he was walking in the garden in the cool of the day, and they hid from the Lord God among the trees of the garden. But the Lord God called to the man, 'where are you?'" (Gen. 3:8–9).

Through the stories of Adam and Eve, Abraham and Sarah, David and Solomon, the entire Hebrew people and their Jewish descendants, through the stories of the life, death, and resurrection of Jesus Christ, and the struggles of the young church, we witness God attempting to build a family and the challenges human sin presents to that process. Human history appears to be a working out of that divine and human relationship. Like childbirth, it is a painful and joyful and exhausting process. There is this wondrous hope for family, while at the same time the immediate concern that the labor will never end.

One of the gifts of the professional pastoral leader is to enter into some of the most intimate moments of people's lives, the joys and deep sorrows that mark the passing of years. One of the most profound pastoral reflections flowing from this experience is that life humbles us all, each and every one of us. There is something about the character of creation that brings us to our knees. The trial and toil of life humbles even the proud and powerful, and we find ourselves before God saying, "O Lamb of God who takes away the sin of the world, have mercy on me." In the end, creation itself does its work and teaches us our place: we are children of God, God's human family. That is our purpose and the core meaning of our existence.

Eternal Life and Resurrection of the Dead

"For God so loved the world that he gave his only Son, so that everyone who believes in him may not perish but may have eternal life" (John 3:16 NRSV). This is easily the most recognizable scripture in the New Testament. It even gets hoisted on placards during field goal attempts at college football games in the United States. If the New Testament were condensed by vote to a single verse, John 3:16 would be the likely winner. It proclaims that, if you believe Jesus is your savior, you will enjoy eternal life with God. Eternal life is arguably the central promise of the New Testament scriptures, right along with the forgiveness of sins, and it is a key component in the creedal affirmations that have defined Christian identity over the centuries.

Human beings are in a bit of a muddle when it comes to the idea of eternal life. Many modern Christians have trouble believing the biblical promise of eternal life, in the sense of an everlasting version of ordinary life, except perfectly free from sin and decay. It strikes such skeptics as suspiciously convenient (as though we are making it up to comfort ourselves) and also objectively unlikely (given the bodily nature of human beings). Life without a body makes no sense in the ancient biblical worldview, so resurrection is essential to enjoy eternal life. Despite this, the widespread and rather unbiblical idea of souls that live without bodies has captured the imagination of many Christians. These folk think of eternal life as immortality of the soul, despite the creedal insistence on resurrection of the dead.

There is another confusing twist, too. Though John 3:16 probably refers to eternal life in the picturesque sense of everlasting life, some Christians have argued that the better meaning is abundant life right here and now, lived in the presence of God (John 10:10), and union with God beyond time after death—not life in a temporal hereafter. This only makes sense, they say, because God is not a temporal being, so eternal life can't be about the passing of time, as it is in the idea of everlasting life. There can be no clocks in heaven.

This intense, timeless union with God is perhaps the most intellectually compelling view but most people probably wouldn't object if the picturesque everlasting-life version of eternal life came true for them. For instance, one of us, though betting that the timeless union with God view is the best one, would love an opportunity in another life to learn to play the cello, and that would take time and physicality and lack of perfection so that there can be room for improvement. A few people might prefer immortality of a nonbodied soul. Some might opt for oblivion rather than enduring the terrifying exhaustion of never-ending life—an impulse deeply related to the Hindu and Buddhist instinct to escape the karmic cycle of rebirth. But there is no question that a perfect version of the life we already know surely is an attractive vision of human destiny for many skeptics and believers alike. In fact, evangelicals typically can't understand why anyone would hesitate to embrace such a wonderful promise.

If the idea of "eternal life" and its connection to "resurrection of the dead" is a bit of a muddle, Paul's view of its importance certainly is not. Paul is as clear as he is adamant in his communications with the Corinthian community. "If there is no resurrection of the dead, then Christ has not been raised; and if Christ has not been raised, then our proclamation has been in vain and your faith has been in vain" (1 Cor. 15:13). If there is no resurrection of the dead then Paul's ministry, Paul's faith, and Paul's churches are worthless. For Paul, faith in Jesus Christ is faith in resurrection to eternal life. The resurrection to eternal life is the means by which the ultimate purpose of creation, namely union with God, is fulfilled. But we can accept that Paul thought it was central without really having a clear idea of what he means by "resurrection of the dead."

Questions always arise when we try to define what eternal life is, what it will look like, and who's going to be in or out. We find Jesus's parables about the kingdom to be instructive on this point. Jesus says the kingdom of God or the kingdom of heaven *is like* a mustard seed, it *is like* a pearl of great value, it *is like* yeast. His parables never venture to say what heaven actually is; he only describes what the kingdom of God *is like.*

So here's where things stand. The promise of eternal life is crucial for making sense of Christian faith. But our contemporary and historic understandings of it are conceptually muddled. It seems we are forced either to throw our lot in with one of the various interpretations of eternal life and reject the others, or to stop talking about it altogether.

We think there is another way. Liberal-evangelical Christians trust God and commit themselves to following Christ. We trust God in this life, and we trust God with eternity. We humbly rec-

ognize that God, heaven, salvation, and eternal life are largely
beyond our imagining. With that said, we trust in the promises
of the Bible because we have thrown our lot in with Jesus Christ
(not with a particular theory of the afterlife). We are committed
to the tradition that has unfolded under his inspiration. We are
committed to the beliefs within that tradition but also to its debates. So we are not afraid of dissenting voices and fierce disagreements, including ones about the meaning of eternal life.
Nor do we shrink from the creative new interpretations that have
nurtured the tradition through its entire history.

We proclaim the resurrection of Jesus Christ and the promise of eternal life because that is *who we are*. We just aren't exactly
sure what Jesus's resurrection looked like, or what eternal life
might look like for us. We know we differ with one another over
how to interpret the resurrection of the dead and eternal life
but we cleave to one another in love with a single hope because
we know *to whom we belong*. We believe in the eternal love of
God and trust that whatever may come—the trials of Job, the
heartbreak of Mary, the death of Stephen—God supports us and
will receive us when we die. We attempt to live lives that will be
worthy of eternal remembrance, and leave the rest to the grace
of God.

A Moderate Conclusion

If you are a moderate Christian of the liberal and evangelical
type, you probably sigh with relief every time you hear a preacher proclaiming the incomprehensibility of divine reality and the
need for theological and spiritual humility. You may feel this
way because of the nausea you experience around overconfident
Christians. But you probably also deeply sense the wonder of
the divine and the smallness of human rational powers to comprehend it. It is both with relief and with joy, then, that you place
your life in the hands of the God of the storm, the God who passes all understanding, and the God in whom we live and move
and have our being.

It is here that we truly begin to see the sense in which a moderate faith of the liberal-evangelical sort can be profound. The most radical faith is not the noisiest or the flashiest but the truest, the one that transforms most deeply, and the one that inspires faithful action most consistently. As strange as it seems, moderate Christians realize how empowering it can be *not* to have God all figured out, and how thrilling it can be to understand God as both discussable and ultimately incomprehensible.

Living out such humility requires work. Liberal-evangelical churches have to stress education, both in the church and in the wider community. The more we know, the better we understand what it means not to know exhaustively what God is. Liberal-evangelical churches also drive home this humble theological awareness through practices that take the focus off of ideas and stress our togetherness as a community—practices such as baptism and the Eucharist, corporate worship and communal prayer. In a different way from education in theological matters, the spiritual practices of the Christian tradition stretch the soul and the mind together. As we learn and live into the complex, contested tradition we inherit as contemporary Christians, we find our place in God's world. We discover how to feel at home in the middle.

PART II

God Was in Christ

CHAPTER 4

Approaching the Gospel Theologically

THE CHRISTOLOGICAL WHIRLWIND

Theological interpretation of Jesus Christ (i.e., Christology) has been the hottest theological flashpoint between liberal evangelicals and conservative evangelicals. It was the most explosive point of debate in the Great Evangelical Split between traditionalist evangelicals and modernist evangelicals at the beginning of the twentieth century (we discussed this in *Lost in the Middle?*), and it was certainly one of the topics on which traditionalists most closely scrutinized modernist writings in the period prior to the split.

The reason for this is fascinating. Certain modernist-traditionalist disagreements were obvious, such as (naming things from the conservative point of view) inerrancy of the Bible, the absolute truth of doctrine, and the separationist social policy whereby the purity of the church was to be protected by withdrawing from social engagement. It was fairly easy to diagnose where writers and speakers stood on these issues. But debates over Jesus Christ were less clear-cut. Jesus Christ was important to everyone on both sides of the evangelical divide and there were intricate ways of speaking about Christology that disguised people's real viewpoints. This forced conservative doctrinal purists to scrutinize every statement about Jesus Christ to decide whether the author in question was orthodox or deviant in faith, from their point of view.

Conservatives often deemed Christ-centered liberal evangelicals to be heretical no matter how biblical their viewpoints simply because liberal evangelicals sought to allow some variation in speculative theological theories of the person and work of Jesus Christ. No variation of opinion was possible for conservative evangelicals; there was one and only one correct way of interpreting Jesus Christ, regardless of how one-sided its biblical credentials were. But liberal evangelicals acknowledged and celebrated the fact that the New Testament contains numerous different attempts to grasp the significance of Jesus Christ. They were more interested in modeling the disciples' relationship to Jesus than in preserving what they saw as an artificial unanimity in the speculative metaphysics of Christology.

There seem to be as many differing beliefs about the identity and significance of Jesus Christ as there are people who have them. James Dunn's classic *Unity and Diversity in the New Testament* gives an excellent survey of the biblical material. Jesus himself is reported to have met with numerous interpretations of his person and work.

> Jesus . . . asked his disciples, "Who do people say that I am?" And they answered him, "John the Baptist; and others, Elijah; and still others, one of the prophets." He asked them, "But who do you say that I am?" Peter answered him, "You are the Messiah." And he sternly ordered them not to tell anyone about him. (Mark 8:27–30 NRSV)

Peter's interpretation, to which Mark seems to give approval in this passage, is what Peter preaches on Pentecost in Acts 2. It is not much like the hypostatic union or Trinitarian theories that unfolded in the ecumenical councils of the fourth and fifth centuries. Evidently the diversity that Jesus seems to have encountered in the period of his own ministry continued through the birth and development of the early church.

In our own context we can trace the diversity of christological views through the code phrases we hear. We call them "code phrases" because they compactly express underlying narrative structures that give the phrases coded meanings. But the underlying narratives are different, in the New Testament as well as in contemporary Christian theology, so we wind up fighting about christological theories through these tell-tale code phrases. Here are some, reflecting quite different underlying salvation narratives.

Jesus is God's only begotten son. Jesus is Emmanuel, the God who enters our human drama to teach us and save us. Jesus is the savior of the world; in fact, no one will enter heaven except through a personal relationship with Jesus. Jesus is the Messiah. Jesus is a good teacher conveying timeless wisdom. Jesus is an important prophet from a long line of Hebrew prophets. Jesus is a social revolutionary enacting convention-defying principles of love, peace, and justice. Jesus is a moral and spiritual example. Jesus defeats Satan in a supernatural battle and human souls are the spoils. Jesus is human. Jesus is divine. Jesus is a little bit of both. Jesus is fully both. Jesus is the second person of the Holy Trinity. Jesus is alive through the resurrection and supernaturally available for personal relationship much like other human relationships. Jesus lives on through being remembered and followed within the communities that bear Christ's name. Or, as a homeless person in Jerusalem shouted out to oncoming throngs of Christian tourists, "Jesus never lived. He is make-believe, like Santa Claus and the Easter Bunny."

Christological code phrases swirl around us, bringing confusion and conflict. The life, death, and resurrection of Jesus Christ is a holy whirlwind that has rattled the windows of millions of individual lives and shaken the very foundations of human civilization. All the creeds in the world could not contain the force of this impact. The staggering potency of the christological whirlwind is an undeniable fact but it can be unsettling. Some respond by cementing a creed in place and adamantly asserting, "Here, this is what we believe about Jesus Christ, and you must believe it too." Others discard the person and work of Jesus Christ altogether, rendering him merely as a recipient or victim of fantastic human longings projected onto his life and activities.

By contrast with these two responses, which we consider short-cuts, we contend that it is truly difficult to make theological sense of the christological facts—and we use the word "facts" advisedly. Enormous numbers of Christians past and present testify that encountering the power and presence of Christ regularly brings light to their darkness and changes the lives of those around them. This is the primal christological experience and the civilizational effects of Jesus Christ flow from it. Those are the facts. The ever-present short-cuts are hazardous. Creedal rigidity distorts the primal christological experience, which is prodigiously varied and not reducible to neat propositions. Reductive psychologizing denies the theological significance of the primal christological experience by claiming that it has nothing to do with the person and work of Jesus Christ, as if any person could have become the reference point for such existential fascination and transformative power on a global scale. Neither short-cut is adequate to the facts.

THE CENTRALITY OF CHRIST

Here's a simple recipe for reducing church vitality: decentralize Christ for Christian identity and focus solely on God. It might take a few years, but the sociological data suggest that it will work for most churches. Plenty of people migrate theologically in just this way in the course of their lives, which is partly why some churches go this way, also. Their inspiration comes partly from aversion to the artificial doctrinal rigidity of conservative approaches to Christology. But it also derives from despair on the left: despair that there is no way to take everything we know from the historical, human, and natural sciences seriously and still maintain a credible claim about the central importance of Jesus Christ.

We contend that this despairing belief is mistaken. We understand the power of historical criticism of the Bible and we feel its impact on our confidence in what the New Testament reports about Jesus's words and actions. We grasp how psychological and sociological explanations of the birth and growth of the Christian movement can undermine confidence in the definitiveness of Jesus Christ for Christian identity. We see clearly the way that core-message pluralism makes many christological statements deeply questionable. Yet we believe *there is a way to articulate a Christian identity that keeps Jesus Christ at the theological center and takes these challenging facts of life with complete seriousness.*

To grasp how this works, we need to understand the stresses and constraints on theological thinking about Jesus Christ in recent centuries. These stress points arise from challenges to christological plot details within large-scale Christian reconciliation narratives. People may worry about a plot detail within a Christian reconciliation narrative and so try to change or ignore it. But even small changes sometimes endanger the underlying story, robbing it of persuasive existential punch. Once we understand the stress points where reconciliation narratives are vulnerable to small changes in plot details, we will also know how to tell a story that makes sense while still honoring everything we have learned from the historical, human, and natural sciences.

NARRATIVE STRUCTURES AND PLOT DETAILS

Intricate stories need many plot details. For example, J. R. R. Tolkien's *Lord of the Rings* crucially depends on the plot detail that the giant eagles absolutely refuse to carry other beings. This is why the problem of taking the One Ring to Mount Doom in Mordor could not be solved simply by hopping on the back of one of the eagles and hitching a ride—perhaps right after the Nazgul had lost their horses and spent months hiking back to Mordor. Send hundreds of eagles if necessary to achieve air superiority. The whole story would be over in a few minutes. If the plot detail that eagles don't carry people is not in place, the strategizing council at Rivendell would seem ridiculous for not at least raising the possibility of flying the ring to Mount Doom, and the entire story would be utterly ruined.

Interestingly, Tolkien flirts with this plot detail both when he has an eagle carry the wizard Gandalf from the top of the tower at Isengard and when he has eagles carry the hobbits Sam and Frodo from Mount Doom after the ring is destroyed. Tolkien must have sensed the danger, because he belabors the eagle's unwillingness to carry Gandalf, but the role of the great eagles really does not make much sense. A plot purist would feel deeply worried that the story was being wrecked because of some self-indulgent little twist and would insist on the elimination of the great eagles, or some similarly effective narrative-protecting move.

This is the way things work with doctrinal purists in Christology. The dominant reconciliation narrative of evangelicalism is not intended to be fictional, of course, nor is it as intricate as *Lord of the Rings*. But it is still richly detailed and it needs to be consistent, so the narrative is vulnerable to changes in plot details. Sadly for the health of the narrative, each of the main plot details has been challenged in the modern period by the rise of historical consciousness and the human and natural sciences. The difficulties in the story are just as threatening to the gospel narrative's coherence as Tolkien's fiddling with the great eagles is to *Lord of the Rings*. And that is why doctrinal purists step up and rigidly insist that *the plot details of the gospel narrative must not change.*

It is important to notice that people tend not to notice the problem with the eagles when they are swept up in the story of *Lord of the Rings*. This trilogy is hailed as a masterpiece partly because it creates its own world of plausibility. Those who inhabit that world are more likely to overlook the problem with eagles and buy into Tolkien's somewhat lame way of managing it. Those who are not captivated by the book can see right through the problem to a deep plot problem and criticize the book in a way that fans wouldn't dream of doing.

The same is true in christological narratives. When we belong to a group whose speech and activities consistently reinforce one christological narrative, the plausibility of the narrative is strengthened. The group's life automatically weaves a spell just as a great novel does, and thereby creates plausibility structures that help to make their christological narrative seem absolutely and obviously true, even though outsiders may find it obviously a mistaken exercise in fantasy and wish fulfillment. The social reality of creating, nurturing, and protecting plausibility structures is what lies behind the various strategies that churches use to handle questions about the coherence of christological theories, and the deepest reason why traditionalists and modernists focused so heavily on the theme of Christology.

The purists are partly correct: changing some details does ruin whatever versions of the reconciliation narrative depend on them. Altering or questioning just one or two key details can break the spell that makes the narrative so unquestionably compelling, and eventually corrode the underlying plausibility structures. No wonder purists are so vigilant about doctrine. From this point of view, doctrinal rigidity is less an expression of personal insecurity or a means of corporate identity formation and more a matter of simple common sense. You don't add plot twists if they wreck the basic logic of the narrative, period. And you can't afford to allow questions about the plot to be raised in ways that destroy plausibility structures, either.

In the next chapter we offer a summary of plot details in the broadly evangelical reconciliation narrative and the corresponding plot twists that threaten to wreck it. As we proceed, we also introduce a number of related but distinguishable reconciliation narratives that play vital roles in contemporary Christian theology and practice.

CHAPTER 5

Gospel Talk

THE HUMAN PREDICAMENT

The broadly evangelical reconciliation narrative posits a predicament: human beings fell (and are still falling). Hindus and Buddhists have a different predicament: human beings are trapped in a karmic cycle of suffering, death, and perpetual rebirth. But in the Christian narrative, the predicament is that human beings became doomed to sin because of a primal decision, the effects of which are transmitted from generation to generation down to today. This is what the biblical version of the Adam and Eve story in the Garden of Eden conveys. To grasp the significance of this primal act for the Christian gospel narrative, note that the Islamic version of the Adam and Eve story in the Qur'an is slightly different. The act of disobedience occurs but God just forgives the mistake and things carry on the way God originally intended. The Islamic story is about submission and obedience in the face of testing, not about overcoming the effects of a terrible *fall* into sin. Anyway, Allah's plans could never be subverted by so small a thing as human disobedience. This interpretation of Genesis is quite different to the one that most Christians tend to place at the beginning of their grand narrative.

The same human condition, the same human weaknesses and sins, are framed very differently in each of these great and world-changing religious narratives. Precisely because the Hindu and Buddhist and Islamic narratives of the human predicament posit a more or less constant situation for human beings, they are better placed than Christianity to cohere with contemporary scientific knowledge. Paleoanthropology—the scientific study of ancient human beings—can't make much sense of the idea of a single primal decision to disobey a direct order from God, which then sets this infection of original sin going. But if you give up the idea of the *fall*, then it seems as though God has to bear a lot of responsibility for creating creatures who sin. It also seems that human beings may not be in such a terrible predicament after all, if they haven't really fallen, and so they wouldn't need Jesus Christ to rescue them. Think about this in terms of plot details. *The Christian reconciliation has to start with the fall in order to make sense of the person and work of Jesus Christ.* Changing this starting point endangers the Christian reconciliation narrative.

The broadly evangelical reconciliation narrative proposes biological and cultural transmission of the fallen state. This is why we can't just leap up from our predicament and solve the sin problem ourselves. While evolutionary biology is quite compatible with the idea of genetic transference of an irresistible urge to selfishness, it can make little sense of the ideas that this state was entered into by a single couple, or that it might not have been entered into at all. But if you give up the idea of forced biological transference of original sin, then it seems as though human beings could educate themselves out of their predicament without any need for special divine intervention. This endangers the narrative.

Interestingly, North African theologian and bishop Saint Augustine went so far as to stipulate a mechanism for the biological transference of original sin. He said it occurred through concupiscence in sexual intercourse, which was a bad thing but tolerable within marriage because the God-ordained purpose of marriage is to procreate. Reading between the lines, it appears that he was using the vague word we translate as "concupiscence" to refer to something much more specific than merely sexual desire, namely, the loss of control in male orgasm. This is uncontrolled concupiscence and, for Augustine, concupiscence was at its very worst when uncontrolled and irrational. This is a bad thing, therefore, but impossible to disentangle from ordinary human nature, and also unavoidable for making babies. The inevitability of male orgasm, and thus of uncontrolled sexual desire, for conception within Augustine's medical outlook reinforced the inescapability of the problem but also provided the perfect mechanism for transmitting original sin.

We now know that Augustine's male-centered implantation view of conception was wrong; the woman provides more biological material to an embryo than the man. We also know that conception can be achieved without male orgasm. So we know Augustine was mistaken. Despite having been quite an important detail in many versions of the salvation narrative for fourteen hundred years, and officially confirmed at the post-Reformation Council of Trent (1545–1563), Augustine's plot detail has now almost completely disappeared from the modern evangelical reconciliation narrative. It is an example of how some plot details can come and go without too much difficulty for the wider narrative structure, given enough time. In fact, this peculiar plot detail not only could fade away without too much damage to the narrative, but it *had to disappear* as broadly accepted medical plausibility structures changed the operative plausibility structures within churches. But something was given up in the process: Augustine's narrative was more tangibly detailed, more sexually loaded (not necessarily in a positive way), and more directly relevant to human morality than the current narrative is. Nevertheless, the reconciliation narrative survives, with an unstated, perhaps supernatural, mechanism for the transference of original sin in place of Augustine's more specific—albeit morally bizarre, medically mistaken, and sexist—proposal.

On top of this, the broadly evangelical reconciliation narrative posits a natural penalty for sin that is truly terrifying. The penalty is pain in childbirth, a recalcitrant Earth that makes agriculture difficult, enmity with other natural creatures, and discord in families (Gen. 3:14–19). Another thread in the narrative makes physical death the ultimate penalty for sin: "The wages of sin is death" (Rom. 6:23). This does not fit with the Genesis account, where death is a natural state and Adam and Eve need to be expelled from the garden lest they further eat from the tree of life and live forever (Gen. 3:22–24). But the narrative as read through Paul's "wages of sin is death" framework is the one that has tended to stick. This narrative suggests that we were naturally immortal beings living in an Eden-like Shangri-la with painless childbirth and an effortless relationship with the rest of nature until original sin placed us in the unnatural situation with which we are completely familiar. Modern science can make no sense of such a Shangri-la. Painless childbirth among human beings is impossible because of the sheer geometry of the situation. Agriculture always involves struggling against and working with nature. Animals behave according to their nature. And death is a part of life, not the enemy of life, just as Genesis suggests. But if you give up the idea of a physical penalty for sin, then you make the cost of wickedness much less tangible and the desperateness of the human predicament much less visceral. This endangers the narrative.

Along with the natural penalty for sin, there is a supernatural penalty in the form of eternal punishment in the flames of hell. That certainly drives home how severe the human predicament is and how desperately any right-minded person should seek to escape it. In this case, the problem is partly theological: would an omni-benevolent God really create a place to consign sinful beings to eternal punishment? But there is also a physical conundrum: where exactly is this place where bodied souls are perpetually tormented? Medieval cosmology used to place these bodies and their torments beneath the surface of the Earth, from which the regular appearance of molten rock once suggested meaningful activity below. Modern people no longer believe that so the narrative now must give the bodied eternal punishment of hell a supernatural framework. Supernaturalists have a lot more to believe these days than was the case in past eras, when so much of the physical world was poorly understood.

Anyway, giving up the supernatural punishment for sin has the same effect that giving up the natural punishment has: the human predicament becomes less dramatic, the motivation for evangelism weakens, and the need for a divine solution to the problem of sin is less desperately urgent. This endangers the narrative. So hell and eternal damnation must be preserved, and the terrifying nightmare of a judgmental deity who deliberately inflicts eternal agony on sinful creatures continues to cast its shadow over the narrative, leveraging prodigious psychic power.

THE DIVINE RESCUE

Against this background of an inescapable human predicament, the broadly evangelical reconciliation narrative posits that God implements a rescue operation to save human beings from their fallen state and to deliver them from the terrible natural and supernatural consequences of sin. This solution is the incarnation, death, descent to hell, and resurrection of God's only begotten son. We'll come to the details in a moment. Right now, there is another theological difficulty.

A perfectly omniscient deity must know that a rescue operation would be needed. This means that incarnation is knitted into creation itself, which pleases theologians, but it also means that God designed the system—even if it is an optimal system—in such a way that some creatures would go to the eternal flames of hell. Calvinism straightforwardly affirms this, with admirable consistency, but many branches of evangelicalism hesitate to treat everything as fulfilling God's intended plan because it appears to lessen human responsibility for sin and makes God seem cruel and cynical. This endangers the narrative. This is a nice example of a coherence tension within the narrative that causes a split among Protestant Christians.

The incarnation is necessary for God's escape plan to work. How so? The best explanation for this plot detail comes from Saint Anselm. He was worried about this plot detail and so wrote a book entitled *Why the God-Human?* Despite the enormous variation in Christian theories of the Great Escape from sin, Anselm's twelfth-century offering seems to be the one that has stuck in the broadly evangelical version of the reconciliation narrative. We'll explain how it goes in several steps.

First, God is perfectly holy. If you offend God by sinning, you have to recompense God by paying satisfaction. There is a medieval honor code at work here; it is not the same as the purity code that underlies animal sacrifice in Jesus's time. Most importantly for Anselm, *God cannot just forgive and forget the way human beings can.* Some people are not pleased with the way Anselm's medieval plot device has inserted itself into the reconciliation narrative. They believe God would not be so rigidly bound by honor

and holiness, and that God could just forgive an earnestly repentant sinner, just as loving parents always forgive a wayward
child who truly repents. But this is the Muslim approach, not the
Christian approach, because it makes the incarnation no longer
necessary for the rescue plan. This endangers the narrative.

Second, sin is so great an offense to God in Anselm's medieval vision of divine holiness that only an infinite payment will
satisfy God's rightful wrath. Unfortunately for them, human beings have no means of paying an infinite moral debt. Even their
very lives would not be enough because the offering would be
stained with sin. Only a perfect human being could make a life
offering sufficient to recompense God for human sin. But original sin guarantees that there is no such perfect human being.
Only God could be perfect. Thus, only a God-man could get the
job done. Full divinity means moral perfection and the possibility of an efficacious sacrifice. Full humanity makes the sacrifice
applicable to human beings.

Given this framework, it is no wonder that conservative evangelicals closely monitor christological pronouncements for any
hint of weakening the "truly human, truly divine" formula. This
is the so-called hypostatic union, referring to the ancient creedal
categories of the fifth-century Council of Chalcedon. When theologians say that Jesus was divine like all human beings are potentially divine, or that Jesus was divine in that he enjoyed a uniquely
strong God consciousness, or that Jesus was divine through being
filled with the Holy Spirit, or that God adopted Jesus as a son because of Jesus's goodness and self-sacrifice, conservative evangelical ears prick up in alarm. They sense that the crisp formulation
of the hypostatic union is becoming soggy and Anselm's reasoning will no longer hold. This endangers the narrative.

Third, for reasons that Anselm does not really explain, the
willing death of the God-man is capable of satisfying the deity
who is so offended by human sin. But the fact that this God-man
is also God's only begotten son has struck people very differently
over the years. To some, including Anselm himself, it seems the
height of love to sacrifice one's own son for the sake of those in
trouble. To others, this is seen as divine child abuse. This latter

group would hastily amend the plot to say that Jesus Christ was himself a victim of human evil, much as Peter says in his first sermon in Acts, and not a willing sacrifice that pays satisfaction for human sin. This latter group thinks that this move rescues the narrative but others believe it endangers the narrative.

The reconciliation narrative contains another reason for why the willing sacrifice of a God-human can succeed as satisfaction for human sin. This detail comes not from Anselm but from much older understandings of animal sacrifice. Just as the blood of animals spilled in sacrificial death could purify human beings before the gods, including Yahweh, the God of the Jews, so spilling the blood of the God-human Jesus Christ could reconcile human beings and the one true God. This is why there are so many evangelical songs about the blood of Christ, or the blood of the Lamb. Being dipped in the blood of Christ is the absolutely necessary condition for emerging purified and free from sin. Those who find this imagery gory and excessive try to change or avoid it. But such changes endanger the narrative.

The narrative also posits a mechanism to make Jesus both truly human and free from original sin. This is an important detail. One key is to avoid a human father who passes original sin through his seed or his orgasm, depending on the mechanics of the medical worldview. This is achieved through the virginal conception of Jesus, whose biology and genetic material come from God alone in the implantation view of conception. In updated medical categories, this means that both egg and sperm must come from God and God alone. The other key is that the house for the pregnancy must be pure. Protestants tend to secure this just through the fact that Mary was a virgin, as if sex were an impure act that permanently defiled a woman. Catholics go much further and posit an immaculate conception for Mary herself, by means of which she is miraculously freed from original sin and can serve as a holy vessel for the baby Jesus. There are plenty of people who don't like this view of sex, or the view of women it supports, or the very idea of the virgin birth, and they advocate what they see as healthy modifications. These changes endanger the narrative.

THE GREAT ENEMY

Note that the reconciliation narrative to this point really has had no need for Satan, thought of as a personal principle of evil. The problem of sin and its solution make good narrative sense without it. But the Christian tradition has nurtured several reconciliation narratives in parallel with the one we have been discussing, and one of these has been integrated into the evangelical gospel narrative while the others have not. We do not refer to the beautiful deification theory of ancient Christianity that thrives in Orthodox and some Catholic circles; Protestants tend to find that appalling because it posits a gradual pathway linking the human and the divine rather than an infinite qualitative distinction between the two. Nor do we refer to the narrative in which Jesus is a Holy Example who heals us as we follow him to our salvation, which is a big theme both in the Bible and in medieval theology, and the most important reconciliation narrative for liberal Christians in our day. No, we refer to the Satan narrative.

The Satan narrative is probably partly inspired by the prologue to the book of Job, in which God and Satan argue about the extent of Job's righteousness and wager over his misery. (There is a related story in the Qur'anic creation narrative in which Iblis is charged with the task of testing human beings.) Just as God hands Job over to Satan for horrific testing and torture, just to prove Satan wrong, so our sin means that we are rightfully under Satan's dominion, destined for eternal punishment in the flames of hell if we don't escape our fate while we are in this life. In this version of the narrative, the incarnate God-human is not paying satisfaction to an offended God but rather redeeming human souls from the devil. The price is the God-human's very lifeblood.

This is familiar to many contemporary Christians through C. S. Lewis's *Chronicles of Narnia,* and particularly *The Lion, the Witch, and the Wardrobe.* Lewis uses this version of the reconciliation narrative as the means by which Aslan redeems Edmund from the possession of the evil White Witch. This narrative structure is also the original source of the word "redemption" in relation to the Christian reconciliation narrative. God "buys back" or redeems souls by paying a price to Satan. The Satan story adds considerable color to the reconciliation narrative, giving it super- natural significance and cosmic dimensions. This is why many evangelicals absorbed it along with the satisfaction story that Anselm so neatly crystallized. Christians who think that per- sonalizing evil in the form of Satan and his demonic minions is surrendering to pagan mythology do not like this narrative and seek to change or ignore it. This threatens the Satan redemption narrative.

Associated with the redemption-from-Satan story is a much grander mythological epic in which good and evil bat- tle for control of the universe. We do not mean anything akin to the *Star Wars* saga, in which the Force and its Dark Side are profoundly entangled and mutually dependent cosmic-moral principles (though this is important in ancient religions such as Manichaeism and Zoroastrianism and also in some forms of re- ligious naturalism). We refer to an epic battle between God and Satan, thought of now quite differently as God's rebellious arch- angel. While this battle plays itself out on a cosmic scale, it often has implications for human beings. The sin and redemption nar- rative is just one of these implications. Others include the idea of demons and angels vying for our moral attention, demon pos- session and exorcism, and the power of the name of Jesus Christ over the satanic powers of hell. The most spectacular implication is a cataclysmic ending to the cosmic story (or is it merely a tran- sition to the next chapter?) that triggers the destruction of human civilization and the world itself. This is the "end-times" story, one version of which the famous *Left Behind* series of novels plays out in exquisite detail. Once again, many evangelicals get worried when people seek to treat angels and demons and cosmic plots as mythological fiction. This endangers the narrative.

THE RESURRECTION

We mention one final narrative detail whose alteration can threat- en the entire broadly evangelical reconciliation narrative. That is the resurrection of Jesus Christ. Notice that we have introduced several parallel reconciliation narratives at this point. The meaning of the resurrection differs depending on the particular reconciliation narrative involved, as we shall see. But it is important in most versions of the story.

In the *redemption* version of the reconciliation narrative, Jesus dies to buy back hapless human souls from the devil's control. But after he dies, Jesus descends to hell and personally defeats Satan in battle before leading the souls trapped there through the gates of hell and upwards into heaven. The resurrection is the humanly comprehensible sign that Jesus's devil-defeating task of redemption is completed. In the *Chronicles of Narnia*, Lewis calls this the "deep magic;" the devil accepts the sacrifice of Jesus for the sake of sinners, thinking that this will give him control over God, but stupidly the devil does not realize this will lead to his own undoing. In the Narnia world, not long after the lion Aslan seals the deal with the White Witch and allows her to kill him, he springs back to life and kills her right back. In the same way, Jesus bursts the bonds of death and rises to life, thereby assuring us that he is the one with control, not Satan. The resurrection is not strictly necessary for victory over Satan and redemption of sinners to make sense, of course. Jesus could have gone straight to heaven with the souls redeemed from hell. But it is a fitting denouement for the narrative, a grand climax that adds huge dramatic value.

In the *satisfaction* version of the narrative (that's Anselm's version), the resurrection is also not strictly necessary. Paying the penalty for sin and satisfying the holy wrath of God makes good sense whether or not Jesus rises to life after his sacrificial death. But the resurrection serves to confirm that God accepts the satisfaction offered through Jesus's sacrifice. The resurrection also shows that God honors Jesus for his willing sacrifice.

In the *exemplar* version of the reconciliation narrative, the resurrection is not absolutely necessary, either. We can follow Christ, carrying our own cross, die as he died, and find ourselves joined with him in the presence of God after death. God offers forgiveness freely to repentant people just as human parents forgive their children. No special redemptions or satisfactions are needed; only repentance and following Christ. Even so, the resurrection can have a special extra role in the exemplar version of the reconciliation narrative: it discloses the hidden nature of human beings. Being a disciple of Jesus Christ means following him not only to death but also through death, to another bodied state of life. This is who we are. And Jesus goes before us to prepare a place for us in that new world.

In the *salvation* version of the story, which we have only mentioned in passing, the emphasis is on healing, as the word "salvation" suggests. Once again the resurrection is not strictly necessary. Jesus's pain and suffering heal our sin-sick souls, and his teaching and example inspire us to live in ways that are more worthy of his healing touch. This all makes good sense whether or not Jesus is raised from the dead. But the resurrection serves to confirm that Jesus in fact has the power necessary to heal the ravages of sin in human hearts.

In the *injustice* version of the reconciliation narrative, compactly presented by the apostle Peter in the account of Pentecost (Acts 2:14–36), the resurrection is *absolutely necessary*. Jesus is murdered by people who believe they are destroying a wicked troublemaker but they actually make the gravest of mistakes. God needs to show which side is right and the resurrection does exactly that. It is the ultimate "I told you so!" God raises Jesus from the dead to show that Jesus now has authority over everyone, including those who killed him. He has been vindicated by God and is rightfully Lord and Master.

Most importantly—and this applies to most versions of the reconciliation narrative—the resurrection manifests the defeat of death. "The wages of sin is death" is a rule that may not seem to apply to Jesus Christ, who was truly divine and free from original sin from the beginning. But the resurrection still serves as a sign for human beings that the death penalty for sin can be removed through faith in the risen Christ. The resurrection becomes a doorway to eternal life for everyone who believes. Without the resurrection, we have no hope that God has overcome the power of death, nor any reason to expect that the penalty for sin has been removed and our slate wiped clean through forgiveness.

Theologians sometimes fudge their language about the resurrection, to the point that it becomes difficult to figure out precisely what they are claiming about what really happened. This irritates conservative evangelicals, who rightly sense that fudging on the reality of a bodily resurrection leads directly to trouble with other elements of the narrative. Many theologians have returned to the Genesis perspective and no longer accept that death is the penalty for sin because they think death is a normal part of life. They don't think that the resurrection is religiously essential because it is not strictly necessary for the reconciliation narrative. This endangers all versions of the reconciliation narrative in which the power of sin is not overcome unless death is also removed.

The various reconciliation narratives we have discussed hold together despite their differences because the plausibility structures nurtured within Christian communities serve as the glue. Outsiders can easily pick holes in the stories and effortlessly point out inconsistencies among the different versions of the narrative. On the inside of evangelical Christian communities, by contrast, these historically and theologically distinguishable narratives are entangled together in a very pleasing way for most people. Like the many strands of a single rope, the stories reinforce one another, or at least they can do so when they are told in the context of a community whose members feel reverence toward them and gratitude because of them. But it does not follow from this that a community can handle unlimited conceptual tensions or inconsistencies. As we have shown, certain plot details matter a lot and changing them can have large effects. Such changes are resisted, accordingly, to maintain the integrity and power of the broadly evangelical reconciliation narrative.

CHAPTER 6

God Was in Christ Reconciling the World

We hope that the previous chapter has made clear the fact that doctrinal purists have a point. There are lots of plot details in the broadly evangelical reconciliation narrative that can't be changed without endangering the intelligibility of the whole. The narrative might change in some details from time to time. Augustine's ancient theory of the biological transmission of original sin was once part of the narrative and is no longer. Anselm's medieval theory of divine satisfaction was once not a part of the narrative and now is. These are relatively small changes but even small changes carry a price. Minimally, it is disturbing to change what is familiar and precious. In our time, the widespread desire to change key details of the narrative in deference to plausibility structures deriving from the historical, human, and natural sciences, or from contemporary moral considerations, threatens to wreck the entire narrative logic.

Liberal Christianity has made many piecemeal changes to the broadly evangelical reconciliation narrative. As in the examples we have given, these changes were prompted by people who find the narrative's plot details implausible or morally questionable, which interferes with their ability to enter into it with enthusiasm and integrity. But the cumulative effect of these changes has been to throw reconciliation narratives into disarray. Human beings love stories and we instinctively know when they make sense and when they don't. We can tolerate some inconsistency and incoherence in our stories, and indeed the Christian story has plenty of that, as our survey of variations in the reconciliation narrative has shown. But certain key details have to remain in place for the broadly evangelical version of the salvation narrative to retain its punch. Liberal Christianity is less appealing to most evangelicals as a result of its coherence-threatening plot adjustments. That is why the doctrinal fundamentals gained such notoriety at the beginning of the twentieth century, and also why many moderate Christians were at one time proud to call themselves fundamentalists (see the discussion of this history in *Lost in the Middle?*).

The hard reality is that even many moderate Christians don't feel fully convinced of all the details of the broadly evangelical reconciliation narrative anymore. This is not due to any lack of faith. It is because they want the reconciliation narrative to feel truly convincing. Too often, the pressure to accept the traditional evangelical reconciliation narrative with no modifications feels to them like a demand to believe ten impossible things before breakfast—it is a kind of mental exercise that really has little significance for genuine religious faith. The view of the world that moderates have absorbed from the historical, human, and natural sciences has enormous explanatory power and emotional appeal for them. Unlike fundamentalists, moderates would very much like their Christian reconciliation narrative to cohere with the modern world picture while still retaining a distinctive message that issues a profound moral and spiritual challenge to their cultural environment.

It has become obvious that making piecemeal changes to the narrative is a more or less disastrous strategy because it leads to a confusing melange of ideas that doesn't hang together. Likewise, entirely new stories (e.g., reconciliation narratives that decenter Jesus Christ, as in Unitarianism, or stories that convert God from omnipotent creator to another creature in the universe with a special but limited role, as in so-called "process theology") challenge the heritage of the faith in a way that moderates often find deeply unsettling. The "let's all celebrate our diverse heritages and salvation stories" is insufficient as a social strategy for bind-ing moderate Christians together (we argued this point in *Lost in the Middle?*). So what are moderates to do?

The solution has many facets, but one facet is crucial: moderates of the liberal-evangelical variety need a reconciliation narrative that explains why Jesus Christ is central to Christian faith. We can't fudge this point. We now know that there are many constraints on this christological account of salvation. But what narrative can satisfy those constraints? We offer such a narrative here. This narrative is true and also deeply satisfying. It has to be learned, like all stories, but it is moving and conveys transformative power by helping its hearers engage God through Christ. It resists the casual dismissal of Christ by the surrounding culture but it also learns from the best of contemporary knowledge. It preaches well because of these characteristics but it also requires us to think.

GETTING THE STORY STARTED

The reconciliation narrative revolves around a biblically inspired catchphrase that theologian D. M. Baillie once used as a framework for his christology: God was in Christ reconciling the world. This coheres intimately with what we earlier called the primal christological experience, namely, that human beings regularly and repeatedly experience grace and transformation through Jesus Christ in a wide variety of personal conditions and cultural contexts. If God is the whence of reconciliation, then Jesus Christ is the hero in a Christian narration of reconciliation. Reconciliation occurs in many ways, not only through Christ, because the Holy Spirit is at work in the world, in every part of nature, in every social circumstance, in every living being, and in each human heart. But the Christian touchstone for understanding this transformative divine work is the person and work of Jesus Christ.

It is in Christ that we see the countercultural force of creative divine love at work in a human context. It is there that we find hints as to the wider work of God in the world. It is through Jesus's words that we receive wisdom to light our steps. We follow in his footsteps because it is in him that we encountered and still encounter the transforming grace of God. Others may engage God differently and we neither resent them for that nor withhold from them our respect, if only because we accept Jesus's saying that that the wind of the Spirit blows where it will and is not subject to our control (John 3:8). But we also recognize Jesus Christ as our Lord and Savior, and it is him that we follow into loving service in the cause of the reign of God.

This beginning to the liberal-evangelical reconciliation narrative is already theologically rich. It carefully acknowledges the manifold ways in which God works, it has deeply trinitarian resonances and suggestions, and it plainly confesses the centrality of Christ for our own saving journey toward God. This makes it broadly ecumenical, consistent with most branches of Christianity, and open to finding God at work in other religious and spiritual traditions. It affirms that Christians have something to share with non-Christians and obliges Christians to learn about God from others. It is also broadly compatible with the contemporary view of the world furnished by the historical, human, and natural sciences.

There are some sharp contrasts with conservative evangelical forms of the reconciliation narrative. The liberal-evangelical story hews close to the line of our own experience—the primal christological experience—and treats speculative theological interpretations of that experience as important but secondary. It displays its heritage in the four New Testament Gospels by placing a discipleship model (following Jesus Christ) ahead of a doctrinal model (theorizing about the person and work of Jesus Christ). Its dialogical and mutually transformative model of evangelism is quite different from the authoritarian model that pays no heed to what the Holy Spirit may be doing in the lives and cultures and religions of non-Christian people independently of Christian missionary efforts. For liberal-evangelical Christians, these are not lapses in faith but biblically inspired reforms. They correct the faith of a church that has sometimes fallen prey to a doctrinal rigidity that vainly and condescendingly attempts to confine God's activity to the processes that lie closest to our own domain of understanding and control.

But this is just the beginning of a reconciliation narrative. The liberal-evangelical story needs more detail. And it is in the details that conflicts among liberal-evangelical Christians arise. We will elaborate the liberal-evangelical story through a series of questions and answers.

THE PROBLEM OF SIN

First, why do we need to be reconciled? From what are we being saved? As usual, liberal-evangelical moderates hew close to the line of experience on this question. Like faithful Christians of every era, they marshal the best understandings of their world to make sense of their experience, and they rely on biblical wisdom to articulate what is religiously significant about it. All of these sources speak with one voice in this instance: sin is a problem. In fact, sin is a vast problem with interlaced personal, social, and spiritual dimensions. Liberal-evangelical Christians are a lot less interested in giving a complicated explanation of how we got into this mess than they are in making sure that human beings take seriously the mess they are in and the disasters of selfishness and stupidity that they continue to cause.

What is the measure of the predicament of sin? Moderate Christians follow the Reformers and some parts of the New Testament on this question: the predicament of sin is so big that we can't extract ourselves from it. God's Spirit works through many social and technological vehicles to increase human health and social justice, and Christians can appreciate those currents in the ocean of divine providence. But sin requires reconciliation with God, also. This extraordinarily simple assertion has great potency. Education, medicine, psychotherapy, and better economic arrangements may well increase social justice and improve the lot of human beings. But to say that God is real is to insist that sin affects the divine-human relationship. Our guilt and shame, our addictions and selfishness, our blind greed and stupidity create and perpetuate injustice and oppression, distort our self-understanding, and ruin our relationships with other human beings, to be sure. But they also destroy harmony with God. Transforming the human condition requires every ounce of human effort but it will never be enough because not everything is in our control. Fundamentally, liberation, salvation, happiness, and peace require reconciliation with God.

This liberal-evangelical account of sin de-centralizes certain elements of the broadly evangelical narrative, particularly a primal sinful decision and biological transmission of a fallen moral state. But the point of those plot elements was to demonstrate that the state of sin was infinitely serious and that human beings could not extricate themselves from it through effort alone. That point is now placed at the very center of the liberal-evangelical reconciliation narrative, and this maintains continuity of essentials with the broadly evangelical narrative. On this view, the core of the narrative is in place and Christians are free to ponder the details. They can affirm a primal sinful decision if they have the worldview to make sense of it. They can elaborate the inevitability of selfishness and violence against an evolutionary background, if they so choose. The liberal-evangelical story can tolerate variation and encourage debate on such speculative questions, so long as the experiential heart and soul of the evangelical narrative remains at the center: sin is an infinitely serious problem that human effort alone can never wholly eradicate. Reconciliation with God is essential and so conversion and being born again into a new relationship with God is the Christian way.

What about the physical penalties for sin in the evangelical gospel narrative? Do "the wages of sin" include physical death? Is overcoming physical death necessary for the overcoming of sin? We think the liberal-evangelical Christian must fight for a holistic understanding of God's creation of the natural world. Everything God created is good, as Genesis 1 repeatedly declares, and that includes the biological world whose complexity absolutely requires birth and death. In another era physical death may have been seen as the enemy of life and the direct result of sin but we believe God made birth and death and life together. To separate them artificially distorts the seamless character of the natural world. Human beings are connected with every living thing through their God-given genetic characteristics and through sharing a planetary ecology of staggering complexity and endless beauty. This is good, very good indeed. The wages of sin are terrible, and often enough include untimely physical death for millions of people who are on the wrong side of economic juggernauts or the horrors of war or needless disease. But sin itself fundamentally kills spiritually, not physically. It kills our spirits through alienating us from our divine ground and source. Human beings find the greatest bliss in the presence of God, so spiritual death is the greatest tragedy.

As with the seriousness of sin, so with the penalties of sin: we think this view of death preserves the heart of the broadly evangelical gospel, and respects its narrative point. Yet it also promotes a much-needed transformation in the way evangelical Christians conceive of death. It frees them to affirm death as a sad but ultimately good and Godly part of life, following Genesis 3:22–24. The result is a view that is more consistent with the natural sciences without weakening the gospel's point about the infinite seriousness of sin and the impossibility of escaping its consequences.

THE PERSON AND WORK OF JESUS CHRIST

If sin is a problem we can attack through effort but never completely solve ourselves, how is the problem solved? God was in Christ reconciling the world, yes, but how is reconciliation achieved through Christ? The cruci-centrism of evangelicalism concurs with the fundamental christological experience at this point: the cross of Christ is central. It is especially because of the cross that Christians feel so grateful and close to Christ, that they pay attention to Jesus's teaching, and that they follow Jesus Christ as Lord and Savior. The Christian way has always been inspired by the picture of a loving savior giving up his life for his followers. It shows how serious the problem of sin is and it makes clear that we need help to extract ourselves from its consequences, to be reconciled with God. Most importantly of all, the cross establishes a personal connection between us and the One who dies; we identify with his suffering.

We have seen that the how of reconciliation—not the fact but the mechanism—has been a point of conflict and endless speculation within Christianity. Speculation began in the early church and the various ideas that were tried out in those early decades appear in the diverse New Testament accounts of the meaning of Jesus's death. Inspired by this example, which is enshrined in the New Testament canon, the speculation has continued right through the history of Christian thought. In this process, the most popular views have often been those that connected with prevailing cultural attitudes about sin and justice. The "unjustly killed but now raised to power" view of the apostle Peter that we have mentioned several times now made sense in the context of a church struggling to articulate itself in an oppressive environment, first in relation to hostile Jewish authorities, and then dangerous Roman overlords. The "sacrificial lamb" view of the book of Hebrews made sense in an era when Jewish Christians were used to animal sacrifices. Anselm's "satisfaction through substitution" view caught on in an era when medieval honor codes dictated when and on what grounds someone could be excused for their offenses. Saint Bonaventure's "exemplar" view rose up within a monastic culture of striving for holiness by following the faithful example of Christ. The "redemption from the devil" view was born and is sustained within worldviews that believe in the reality of Satan not just as a tempter but also as one who holds dominion and power over sinners. Rudolph Bultmann's and Paul Tillich's "demythologized existential" view became appealing in an era when people believed that religion had to be about the meaning of the here and now.

Despite this diversity of speculation around the how of reconciliation, Christians of almost all stripes agree that the cross is central, that reconciliation is the final goal, that reconciliation is through Christ, that God was in Christ, and that our experience of reconciliation with God through Christ—what we are calling the fundamental christological experience—is so powerful that it has to be taken with the utmost seriousness as constraining our theological reflection on the how of reconciliation. That is a solid starting point. We do well to recognize what disagreeing Christians actually have in common before getting lost in the theological fights over which speculative reconciliation theory is superior.

Confronting Christ with Christological Speculation

Some Christians get sick and tired of all the abstruse theological speculation in reconciliation narratives and just want to focus on following Jesus Christ. Such folk love the following joke, which plays off of Mark 8:27–30.

> Jesus said: "Who do you say that I am?"
>
> The disciples answered, "You are the eschatological mani-festation of the ground of our being, the transformative ker-ygma in which we find the ultimate meaning of our personal relationships."
>
> And Jesus said, "What?"
>
> Then Peter answered, "You are the paschal lamb who is to be sacrificed so that God will be entitled to forgive our sins, or else so that God can build the capital needed to buy back our souls from the devil; we're not sure. Either way it looks bad for you."
>
> And Jesus said, "You must be kidding."

That perfectly captures how seminary students often feel on encountering the diverse ways that theologians have struggled to make sense of the how of reconciliation. Only a few get excited by all the speculation. Most think that the right answer ought to be something that Jesus himself can understand; it should be timeless, not trendy.

Notice how the frustrated seminary student (in the voice of Peter) imaginatively connects with Jesus over the hard, hard fact that he must die. That's often what matters most to pastors-in-training when they come to theories of reconciliation. They want to make all the abstractions real by connecting them personally with Jesus. They seek to test the abstract theology by seeing how it fares when they imaginatively look Jesus in the eye and tell him about it. It is a fabulous irony that seminary students turn to Jesus as a comforting retreat from theological speculation about why Jesus is important for reconciliation.

Theological reflection is important. It orients Christians to their faith and brings understanding of what the church affirms. It satisfies curiosity and enables us to engage God with our minds as well as our emotions. Theology also plays a vital role in the church as a vast institution with all of the needs for identity and flexibility that social institutions have. Seminary students might find it difficult when they first meet serious theology but most of them adjust eventually. The seminary student's longing for simple answers to doctrinal questions is misplaced; life is not like that. But the worry that we might get overly attached to our favorite theological speculations, after which we are tempted to pick fights with people who do not see things the way we do, is right on the money. And that is especially true in theories of the how of reconciliation.

From Doctrine to Discipleship

So how do we proceed from the solid starting point described above in such a way that we do not fall prey to speculative enthusiasm, suffer from ignorance of alternatives, or lose sight of Jesus himself? The basic answer is to shift from a doctrinal model to a discipleship model. Instead of making Jesus Christ primarily an object of theological reflection, we make following Jesus Christ the primary thrust of theology. That means we imaginatively picture ourselves in the position of his disciples, trying to sort out how to live our lives in the presence of this prodigiously compelling spiritual master and teacher and friend. It means that we recognize the fundamental christological experience as the basis for a relationship, not just a wellspring of doctrinal convictions. It means that we cling to Christ rather than doctrine when people we love and respect—or can learn to love and respect—think differently than we do about how reconciliation works.

The spiritual posture of following Christ opens us up to the whole history of Christian thought and practice surrounding the experience of reconciliation. Once we see that all followers of Christ have reconciliation in common, it is easier to empathize with their culturally specific theories about how it works. The history of Christianity links us to forbears in the faith with very different ideas about reconciliation than we prefer—no matter what our favorite ideas of reconciliation are. We can picture ourselves following Jesus in his band of disciples, each with our own ideas but all focused on him. This is the liberal-evangelical ideal: freedom to interpret joined with devotion to Christ.

We have suggested that there are limits to the interpretative flexibility of the "God was in Christ reconciling the world" gospel. It has to be Christ-centered and cross-centered. It has to place following Christ ahead of doctrinal speculations about Christ's person and work. And it has to stay close to the primal christological experience of reconciliation with God. In other areas there is some flexibility. Here are a couple of questions on which we think liberal-evangelical Christians can legitimately disagree.

First, is God free to forgive sin apart from the person and work of Jesus Christ? This is a contentious point in the history of Christian doctrine because to say that God cannot forgive freely is to limit God's power. Yet to say that God can forgive freely seems to limit the necessity of the incarnation and the cross. No wonder theologians have gone in both directions on this question. Anselm argues on the basis of his medieval culture's honor code that God is not free to forgive sin without a substitutionary atonement. Aquinas argues the opposite, saying that God, through the divine Spirit, may be taking saving action that is beyond our knowledge and experience, but that our knowledge and experience of reconciliation with God comes through Christ. Given what we said in the first chapter about the God of the storm far surpassing human cognitive grasp, we lean toward the latter view, but we see no problem worshiping and following Christ alongside fellow disciples whose metaphysics allows God somehow to be limited in power or in willingness to forgive.

Second, does a Christ-centered account of reconciliation require a supernatural worldview? Most of the Christian tradition has had supernatural worldviews of various types and it is only in the last several centuries that some theologians have tried to

frame the gospel in terms more compatible with the modern scientific view of the world. But we think reconciliation with God
through Christ makes sense on both sorts of worldview, even
though some of the key terms have different meanings. In fact,
one of us operates with a supernatural worldview and the other
does not but we are both followers of Christ and both of us experience reconciliation through Christ. The supernatural world
picture permits us to picture Christ as a living entity right now,
literally with us and actually communicating to us. Meanwhile,
the non-supernatural worldview relies on the biblical portrayals
of the life and teaching of Jesus to engage God. Some Christians
are strongly drawn to one or the other, and a few are deeply offended by the one they don't like. But the actual experience of
following Christ is quite similar whether or not a supernatural
worldview is in play.

THE MEANING OF SALVATION

Evangelical Christians have a formula for salvation. Liberal
Christians say there is no formula when grace is at work. Evangelical Christians say, "Follow Jesus." Liberal Christians say,
"Follow your heart." While there may be little agreement among
moderate Christians about what salvation is, there is no way to
ignore the centrality of salvation in the Bible, particularly in the
New Testament. "If you declare with your mouth, 'Jesus is Lord,'
and believe in your heart that God raised him from the dead, you
will be saved" (Rom. 10:9 TNIV). Paul preached salvation in these
terms to much of the Mediterranean world. David cried out for
salvation in the Psalms. Jesus taught salvation in his parables.
In the Hebrew Bible salvation often had a worldly quality to it.
People cried out for God to save them from the trials and snares
of this life. In the New Testament, salvation is an otherworldly
affair. To be saved is to inherit eternal life.

For evangelical Christians, getting saved and making sure
one's family and friends are saved are of paramount importance.
A critique of some evangelicals, often expressed by other evangelicals, is that they are so intently focused on the afterlife that

they shirk their responsibility to work for peace and justice in the here and now. Many liberals emphasize social action and, as a result, they tend to play down talk of salvation and a life hereafter. Many liberals have grown up in conservative churches and were well acquainted with the God who was ready at a moment's notice to fling us into the depths of hell with its unquenchable fire. The Christian faith was an awesome thing with fearful dimensions. As they matured in faith, these folks rebelled against their conservative Christian upbringings, yet their faith was still important enough to them to remain in church. Many other liberal Christians waver right on the line of universalism. They believe God is love, and if God is love then God will "save" everyone, whatever that means, so why spend time obsessing about salvation? However this discord in views of salvation shows itself, salvation remains important to the Christian faith.

For moderate Christians there is a great hope that is tempered by the humility of which we have already spoken. They believe that all Christians, as well as all of God's human family, can and should work intelligently and passionately for the salvation of this world. Salvation comes through clean drinking water. Salvation comes when weapons of mass destruction are dismantled. Salvation comes when nations with food in abundance share food and agricultural technology with nations that are gripped with famine. Salvation comes in the reorganization of economic systems that are wrongly geared to maintain large differences between rich and poor. Salvation comes when faith in Christ breaks the power of sin and reconciles human beings to God. In the end, we trust the God who set creation in motion, the God who is the ground of our being, the God who is the whence of reconciliation wherever it occurs, and the God whom Christians encounter in Christ's reconciling life and death, to take care of us in this life and beyond.

A MODERATE CONCLUSION

If you are a moderate Christian of the liberal and evangelical type, you may be delighted to know that there is a compelling gospel narrative that fits both your faith and the Bible, both reason and tradition. This gospel message respects the Christ-centered and cross-centered elements of evangelicalism and honors the fundamental christological experience of reconciliation with God. Yet it does not insist that every speculative plot device in the conservative evangelical reconciliation narrative be taken at face value. Having become used to avoiding talk about the actual content of the gospel for fear of disagreement, you may sense dawning relief that it might be possible to talk about your faith, hold fast to evangelical essentials, and not get derailed by disagreement over inessential details. That is what the liberal-evangelical gospel narrative is all about.

We have said that this gospel narrative preaches. Indeed, this was the viewpoint of some of the greatest preachers of the twentieth century, from Horace Bushnell and William Newton Clarke to E. Stanley Jones and Harry Emerson Fosdick—all firmly within the liberal-evangelical tradition. But, like all aspects of the Christian faith, this message also needs to be learned. This is where religious practices enter the picture. Liberal-evangelical Christians need to know the reconciliation narrative well enough that they can see what is indispensable in it and become comfortable with disagreement on inessential points. To do this, liberal-evangelical churches need programs of supportive Christian education to articulate this gospel narrative. Such programs can create both the confidence and the courage needed to talk honestly about faith. Liberal-evangelical churches also need spiritual practices to help activate this way of thinking about the Christian gospel in lives of prayerful service.

Pluralism of belief does not require Christians to remain silent in church about traditionally controversial issues such as the gospel narrative. Rather, it invites them to learn about the core-message pluralism of the Bible and early Christianity, and thereby to understand how pluralism of belief can be perfectly compatible with a compelling, Christ-centered gospel of reconciliation.

PART III

Choosing the
Sugar-Shack Church

CHAPTER 7

The Practical Problem of Pluralism

Moderate Christians intuitively grasp after a socially radical form of Christian faith. Their congregations must adopt a social strategy that flies in the face of sociological odds, if they are serious about radical inclusiveness that transcends extant variations in theology and political ideology. These individuals are willing to embrace the inconvenience of theological pluralism and ideological conflict in order to testify to divine love. They see this as part of their calling to be followers of Christ because that is what he did in his ministry.

This chapter is about the challenge of such a Christian lifestyle, about how churches manage pluralism of opinion and moral intuition, of politics and theology. We take a broadly ecumenical and ecclesiological perspective. But the rubber meets the road in individual communities of faith, in each encounter between people who disagree, and in every feeling of frustration and disappointment. How do moderate Christians demonstrate God's love in those moments? How should they manage failures of love and unity?

CHURCH SHOPPING

The phenomenon of church shopping has inspired church marketing strategies that intelligently pitch the "religious group experience" to target audiences. Our interest is not in marketing for sociologically predictable growth, however, but in a fascinating pattern that defies large-scale church-shopping trends. It is this: some moderate Christians deliberately look for a challenge when they go church shopping. They want friendship, energy, identity, orientation, and purpose in their chosen congregation, it is true, and in those ways they are like other church shoppers. But they also want to be part of a church that sends a strong message of unity to the divided culture around them, and a spiritually potent message to a society addicted to superficiality. They seek a church community that unites different kinds of people in a shared journey of Christian discipleship. They church shop, yes. But they are discerning customers. They are seeking what we call liberal-evangelical churches, even if they don't have words for it.

Church shopping is a merger of a consumerist mentality with the variety of Christian worship and service lifestyles. We can construct a picture of this still emerging phenomenon using surveys from organizations that study Christians and Christian churches such as the Barna Group and the Alban Institute.

In an average U.S. city, even without traveling far, and even after ruling out forms of Christianity that seem thoroughly alien, a serious church shopper might confront a dozen intriguing options. The era before the baby boomers grew up enjoyed stronger denominational loyalty than we see now. A family moving into a new area would typically use the telephone directory to locate the nearest church of their denomination, contact the minister, and transfer their membership. These days, while most Christians still identify themselves with a denomination, the consumerist habits of boomers and their children have taken over.

This means that people look for church homes first using the Internet to gather data. Forget about the telephone directory and newspaper advertisements. After personal recommendations from friends, a church's Internet presence is the leading factor in making first contact with prospective "buyers" of the younger generations. Some use the web to make sure a congregation passes "litmus test" criteria: if they have the wrong view on gay marriage, or salvation, or other religions, or the second-coming of Christ, or baptism, then just rule that church out and move on. Most use the web to get a feel for what it might be like to visit the church. No surprise there. Most church shoppers report that they are looking for a spiritual experience and a lifestyle, more than specific doctrinal beliefs.

Visitors to a congregation have diverse priorities. They may evaluate music, preaching, congregational energy, friendliness, child care, or opportunities for meaningful service. If they come back, it is to get a closer look—to try before they buy. When they finally make a "purchase" decision, most have little "brand loyalty" and need to be "resold" on their decision to avoid "buyer's remorse." If they feel unhappy with their "purchase" they may "trade up" to another "model." In fact, more than two-thirds of first-time church shoppers are active members of another congregation. One in seven people changes churches in any given year. It seems that most church shoppers are unhappy and looking for a better spiritual fit.

It is impossible not to feel a little dismayed at the extent of church shopping, particularly if you think church involvement should be a lifelong act of commitment that takes you through good times and bad, like marriage and family. The statistic that two-thirds of first-time visitors are active members of another congregation suggests that people would rather move somewhere new than work through a difficulty in their old church. A convenient marketplace of church options has made tolerating people with different opinions and personal styles something of a lost art. Why fight for unity in the face of diversity when you can just move on to another congregation?

REVOLUTIONARY CHRISTIANS

Parallel to the frustrations manifest in church shopping are the frustrations of so-called revolutionary Christians. According to George Barna's research, these Christians are very serious about their spirituality but deeply dissatisfied with the ability of local churches to support and nurture an intense and demanding life of faith and service. Revolutionary Christians strive to *be church* even when they find it difficult to *attend church*. They are bored with churches and long for intimate worship, conversation about their beliefs, deliberate spiritual growth, an experience of servant ministry, focused resource investment, spiritual friendships, and family faith. This "movement" began spontaneously in the mid-'80s. According to the Barna Group, it now numbers twenty million in the United States and is growing quickly. This grouping does not show up on surveys (such as the General Social Survey) that do not specifically set out to count them because many revolutionary Christians have a loose affiliation with one or another church and get counted under that category.

Barna thinks that this group of passionate Christians defines the Third Great Awakening and argues that it will profoundly change the religious landscape of North America. We are not so sure. But there is no question that revolutionary Christians are a large and diverse group. Indeed, one of us belonged to an independent house church for several years and took this as his primary Christian identity. The experience remains seared into his imagination, defining standards for Christian faith and friendship that he has rarely seen since. We understand first-hand who Barna is describing as revolutionary Christians. We think his research suggests that their ranks are swelled by some who would be liberal evangelicals in the way we use this term—people frustrated with both of the well-defined ends of the Christian spectrum and yet determined to follow Christ in a radically inclusive way.

SHOPPING FOR A CHALLENGE

While most church shoppers are looking to leave frustrating situations, it is noteworthy that some deliberately seek out congregations with awkward pluralism of opinions or values, of race or culture, of theology and spirituality. They actually *want* the challenge of fighting for unity in the face of diverse doctrines and cultural traditions. They use church shopping to locate a place where they can take a stand against customized religion, against congregations of convenience, and against churches whose understanding of Christian discipleship seems to begin on the wrong foot—with the ideal of comfort through like-mindedness, and with an identity driven by a refined marketing strategy.

This resistance to easy comfort in religion is a common view among moderate Christians. For them, Saint Paul's analogy "body of Christ" (1 Corinthians 12) means that the church should be united, not unanimous. It means that everyone has a role, not that everyone has the same regimented spiritual style. There is nothing more countercultural than to resist the endless catering to taste and preference that a consumerist culture promises.

In a society torn by ideological battles and catering to every individual whim, the most prominent shared values seem to be economic. We accept the economics of consumerism because it enables very different people to satisfy most of their needs and desires without having to fight each other over fundamental values and beliefs. The American experiment in pluralistic society would be difficult to imagine without an economy that makes life interesting and convenient, that keeps Americans apart just enough so that they can still stay together as a nation.

It is easy to appreciate peace and economies that make for peace. No parent wants to fight for food to feed a child. But this low-energy, economically driven unity instinctively worries some people. It seems too much a matter of convenience and thus too unstable to see us through hard times. They seek a higher and more robust unity through love and acceptance of the different and difficult Other. They want their churches to model those qualities for the rest of society. When these people go church shopping, they are not looking for just the right kind of evangelicalism or liberalism. They do not prize above all else unanimity on doctrines and social values. Rather, they seek a community that testifies to the power of love and acceptance in the face of pluralism of opinion and practice, race and culture. They want to commit their lives to modeling a better way for Christian discipleship in a consumerist culture.

In a Small New England Village . . .

In a town we know, a person has four options for church attendance. You can attend the Unitarian church on the town green, you can try the Catholic church on the busy commercial street, you can make your way to the latest evangelical church in the nearby industrial park, or you can attend the United Church of Christ, which was built to look like an oversized New England sugar shack.

The first three churches are what you might expect. The Unitarian church is adorned with a rainbow flag marking it as a safe place for gay and lesbian people. The marquee outside the church proclaims a quote from Henry Thoreau. Inside the congregation is grey and small, and yet impeccably dressed. The sermons are typically anti-war, anti-poverty, anti-Republican, and often conclude with an Emerson poem. You are more likely to hear the words of the Dalai Lama than the words of Jesus Christ. Jesus language makes most Unitarians uncomfortable: half of them think it is too one-sidedly Christian and the other half don't want to offend the first half. But the building looks great thanks to the donors who generously supported the original endowment two hundred and thirty-seven years ago. The coffee hour after worship lasts over an hour as members warmly greet one another and chat about their families and discuss key points from the sermon. A few folk cluster with the property committee in a corner to discuss having the sanctuary repainted a satin cream color to match the bulletin covers. People keep coming back because this way of finding, celebrating, and nurturing spiritual depth in modern life truly suits them.

Just past the McDonald's and the Friendly's Restaurant you find the Catholic church. It is flanked by two giant parking lots marked not with individual parking spots, but with long parking lanes for a quick and easy getaway after Mass. The church service is packed with people of every age. Children squirm and scream in the pews and no one seems to mind. The liturgy is performed, there is a homily having something to do with a letter the archbishop recently sent to all the churches, an offering is taken, communion is given and received, and then there is the mad dash to the cars. With only passing words of greeting between friends, worshipers exit the sanctuary like cattle released from the barn. People keep coming back because this way of forging a community, families gathered around the eucharistic sacrament, is in their blood and precious to them.

The evangelical church housed in the industrial complex lacks some charm, but people are greeted before they get out of their vehicles. Everyone smiles. They all wear name tags. New people are welcomed like long lost brothers and sisters. Worship begins with forty-five minutes of singing led by a high-quality band with the lyrics projected for all to see. Cultural high-brows might not like them but the songs are catchy—the tunes can stick in your head for days. The church seems fun and lively. The people holding their hands in the air and the crying worshipers can seem a bit odd. But everyone is so friendly, and the pastor in the denim shirt with his sleeves rolled up preaches a sermon that makes the Bible seem as though it might actually apply to everyday life. After the sermon, visitors and new people start making their way up to the front, along with a group of regulars who love the altar call. The pastor prays for them, and then they are ushered into a separate room where trained church members try to persuade the newcomers to accept Jesus Christ as their personal savior and special prayers are offered for the regulars. A lot of people show up each Sunday at this church because of the liveliness of the worship, because they understand what is said and done, and because they can feel their faith growing when they get together.

The sugar shack UCC church is a bit of an oddity. At first glance, the green mold on the exterior of the church suggests a congregation in financial struggle. But the church is bustling inside. The buzz about this church is that it is evangelical, and yet liberal at the same time. It is a Protestant church, but like a Catholic church it serves Communion every Sunday. Gay and lesbian folk are welcomed as they are, but the pastor is always preaching about following Jesus Christ. Evangelical Christians attend this church, as well as Unitarian Christians and many disillusioned Catholics. The church is committed to personal holiness, and yet it operates social service missions throughout the world. The youth groups are vast, and yet meetings are not just popular social gatherings but also opportunities for prayer and Bible study and discussion. Republicans and Democrats fill the pews and disagree openly, and yet they return each Sunday. Initially, it appears to be a kind of schizophrenic church that can't make up its mind about what it believes. Yet it feels like a unique place where people can engage their hearts without having to check their minds at the door. People keep coming back, fascinated, with the sense that something worthwhile is afoot.

Some church shoppers make the sugar-shack church their home. They feel welcome, and they love the energy and programs, the biblical preaching and the weekly Communion. But they also find something less tangible, something they instinctively recognize: a spiritual calling to manifest unity in diversity. Not everyone wants this exciting and stressful form of Christian unity, preferring the comfort of a spiritual home with more like-minded members—like the other three churches in town. But some seek out the challenge. They feel called to be a part of a church that breaks cultural habits of suspicion across racial and economic and ideological lines. They commit themselves to manifesting unity and love that makes Christ present in a radically inclusive way. They fight at meetings when they need to but they begin and end each meeting in prayer, together. They put following Jesus Christ first so that, with their eyes fixed on Jesus and their hands busy with Christ's work, their disagreements with fellow disciples are tolerable, secondary.

We are fascinated by the sugar-shack church. We have sought to understand the possibility it represents: some churches can decide to—and do—transcend the liberal-versus-evangelical divide. We have tried to understand its solution to managing diversity, the principles guiding its decisions, the narratives structuring its identity. We have pondered why some church shoppers feel strongly called to embrace its corporate life as their context for Christian growth and discipleship.

We have also made an effort to grasp why some people find this kind of church unattractive or even a pernicious betrayal of Christian truth. Surely it is obvious that not everyone *wants* to find unity among Christians of different stripes, and especially across the liberal-versus-evangelical divide. But it is extremely important to see that such unity is *possible* for those who choose it, so long as they have the right kind of support. For discerning Christians, this is the better way and a higher calling. And we suspect it is becoming more common as the vast group of moderate Christians becomes restless with the perils and stupidities of culture wars and political polarization.

CHAPTER 8

Transcending Pluralism: The Classic Formula

The social reality of theological and spiritual pluralism reminds us of a pair of old maxims: "different strokes for different folks" and "birds of a feather flock together." The social response to pluralism begins with recognition of difference and then develops through the flocking together of similar people to minimize fighting (we discussed this in detail in *Lost in the Middle?*). But where does it go after that basic form of tribalism? Is there a well-defined Christian attitude to theological, political, moral, and spiritual pluralism in the churches?

FLOCKING

The early nineteenth-century German theologian Friedrich Schleiermacher noticed the pluralism issue and the diverse flocks of people that exist in response to it. He approved of this, believing that being with spiritually similar friends helps a person grow in faith. Importantly, he did not confine his approval of this to theological abstractions. There is a story about Schleiermacher when he was a well-known pastor in Berlin. His much younger wife, Henriette von Willich, confided to him that she found his sermons ill-suited to her spiritual tastes (they were probably a bit heady). Now, in those days the wife and children of a German Protestant minister were expected to be in the front pew every Sunday, faithfully supporting their pastor husband and father. So it was no small thing for him or his congregation when Friedrich suggested that Henriette attend the services and hear the sermons of his colleague in the church down the street, which Friedrich thought would suit her better. Schleiermacher was committed in practice as well as in theory to the flocking of like-minded people in the face of spiritual pluralism.

Two hundred years later, the flocking principle is still the most immediate response to the reality of spiritual and theological pluralism. That is why there have been diverse Christian options throughout the Western world during the last five hundred years, as well as in many places and periods prior to the Reformation. The flocking principle applies in China and Korea and Africa as well as in the United States and Europe and Australia. This social reality is the perennially fertile soil into which the seed of contemporary consumerism falls. After that it is not long before we are faced with a tangled weed of a plant: consumerist church culture, rampant church shopping, and rapid reaffiliation when something does not feel quite right about one's home church.

We find fault with theological attacks on consumerist culture if they propound an ideal of Christian loyalty that ignores the fact of longstanding pluralism within Christian churches. Such attacks are historically inaccurate and sociologically unrealistic. Like-minded people have always flocked together, in different parts of a congregation if not in different churches. Nevertheless, the consumerist mentality is a blight on the Christian church and a kind of spiritual sickness. It is partly this sickness that many of Barna's revolutionary Christians are fleeing. Thus, it is not surprising that many ordinary Christians resist the church shopping instinct and try hard to remain loyal to their congregations even if they don't feel completely at home there. It seems that Schleiermacher's flocking principle is complemented in practice by another principle: persevering in loyalty to the integrity of the body of Christ.

PERSEVERANCE

The flocking principle and the perseverance principle are both important elements in any understanding of North American Christians in our time. It has always been so, in large and small ways, throughout the history of the church. In other places and times, the divisions between Christian "brands" have been so severe and "brand loyalty" so strong that it was very difficult to shop around. Rigid class and subculture loyalties prohibited intermarriage, shared worship, and sometimes even commerce between members of different Christian groups. Often there was only one church in a medieval village and the authority of the priest or pastor was a unifying force. But the flocking principle was still evident in such situations. Within the substructures of each church, different kinds of people gathered to undertake preferred activities. Some made meals, some maintained the buildings, some raised money, some prayed together, some made music, some helped the sick and infirm. The same is true whenever the perseverance principle is dominant: flocking still occurs within the variegated structures of the body of Christ.

The New Testament recognizes that spiritual flocking inevitably occurs. Early church history makes clear that ancient Christians had diverse opinions and preferences and that the resultant flocking caused unity problems. Church unity is fine in principle but, when people get to know one another well, they discover that they really are quite different. They begin to fight over group priorities, moral superiority, and institutional control. They band together in supportive groups. The experience of this reality in the early church led many New Testament writers to emphasize perseverance in the Christian life. We read that we should train hard (1 Cor. 9:24–27) and run with perseverance the race that is set before us (Heb. 12:1).

In his meditation on the body of Christ (1 Corinthians 12), the apostle Paul stressed that many kinds of people with diverse abilities and interests should have a place within the church. According to him, we should be confident in our role, whatever it is, and understand that we exercise our divinely given gifts for the sake of others, to whom we are responsible, and for the sake of

Christ, to whom we are loyal. It is through our different gifts that we find a home as servants in the church and the church finds unity in diversity.

Paul's reflection on inevitable differentiation and perseverance within the body of Christ is not an unaccompanied solo. The Apostle adds two other voices. He insists each person be *humble* about his or her role and that each have *empathy* with those who have different inclinations and callings. We all know from personal experience that these are wise and necessary injunctions. Things can go badly wrong when we neglect humility and empathy. We also know, by contrast, how satisfying it is to rejoice together and to encourage one another.

HUMILITY

The principle of humility recognizes that life is complicated, human wisdom is always partial, and divine reality is beyond human comprehension and control ("For now we see in a mirror, dimly" (1 Cor. 13:12). We have no business pretending otherwise but somehow we find ourselves doing just that.

Seminary students and ministers are particularly vulnerable to this lapse of good judgment. They are the dedicated experts of the Christian churches, the ones who typically know the most and have trained the hardest intellectually and spiritually for their leadership roles. All that work must mean they know more than other people, right? Well yes, of course, in some respects. The authority given to the pastoral and priestly role reflects the church's need for well-prepared ministers. They have to possess profound and practical knowledge of theology and philosophy, of Bible and history, of psychology and pastoral care, of church administration and denominational polity. But most ministers realize that having more specialized training than the average parishioner does not confer spiritual superiority—a point that may be lost on many parishioners.

Spiritual insight into the ways of God comes slowly to the devoted and observant soul, to the loving and faithful servant of Christ who resists fixity of mind for the sake of wisdom and who refuses comfortable dullness of heart for the sake of compassion. There are so many reasons to be humble in this world of ours that we really have to adopt a sullen ignorance to miss them. Older Christians should model humility for younger Christians, because it is especially when we are young that our lack of experience of life's complexities leaves us vulnerable to arrogance.

For Christians, in the final analysis, humility is our calling because it was Christ's. Paul makes precisely this point in arguing that Christians should not fight with one another because they should be humble as Christ was humble (Phil. 2:1–11). The definitive expression of humility is baptism, which all Christians share in common (1 Cor. 12:13). In this way, humility is welded to gratitude. We know we have no claim on divine mercy but God's grace reaches out to us anyway. Arrogance is impossible in the presence of simple gratitude for divine acceptance. Nothing unites warring church factions more quickly than a disaster that reminds us that we have so much to be thankful for, and reestablishes humility in place of self-protection, self-denial, and self-promotion.

EMPATHY

The principle of empathy is equally difficult to embody. Humility helps, of course, but no matter how humble and grateful you feel, it is truly painful being on the wrong end of someone else's intolerance, and that is a serious challenge to empathy.

Paul was on the wrong end of the Judaizing party of early Christianity, which insisted against Paul that Christians had to be Jews, and if they were not already Jews then they had to be circumcised and become Jews. For them the idea of a non-Jewish Christian was a contradiction in terms. They had serious reasons to fight with Paul and others who wanted to let Christianity spread beyond its original Jewish cultural and religious framework. From their point of view, the integrity of Christ's message was at stake. Jesus was a Jew and, as he himself is reported to have said, he came only to the Jews (Matt. 15:24). Paul was ruining everything. He was advocating cultural compromise and impurity of the gospel! So the more fervent among these Christian brothers and sisters hunted and repeatedly beat Paul to within an inch of his life (2 Cor. 11:22–28). Under such brutal treatment, Paul must have remembered his old life as Saul, and how he had had hunted and beaten and imprisoned and killed Jewish Christians for betraying the teachings of Judaism by following Christ (Acts 7:54–8:3, 9:1–5).

Everyone always has reasons for intolerant and violent behavior. Rationalizations are easy to invent for quickly frustrated and terribly smart creatures like us. But the rationalization for empathy is equally compelling. On the pragmatic side, violence and hatred make everyone miserable and fuel a circle of aggression and retribution. On the spiritual side, love requires tolerance and a wholehearted attempt to understand those with whom we disagree. We are not called to surrender our convictions to keep other people happy. But we are called to empathize with differently minded others in love. Paul drives the point home: to avoid chaos in the body of Christ, we are to care for each other, despite our different opinions and roles. If one of us suffers, then we all suffer, and if one is honored then everyone rejoices (1 Cor. 12:25–26).

Tolerance, it must be pointed out, is not the same as empathy. Should the unwilling slave tolerate the master's politics? Should women tolerate patriarchal ecclesial authority? Should gays and lesbians tolerate the person who condemns them to hell because of who they love? They do not and should not. The prophetic voice of the church is as important within the church as it is when the church must take a stand against an element of its cultural environment. To make prophetic judgments means to decide not to tolerate. But empathy reaches across necessary lines of judgment, complicating neat classifications of good and evil.

Empathy shows us what those we resist most deeply treasure and most intensely fear. It is almost impossible for most people to empathize with those whose policies and politics they hate. But Christians have a higher calling than most people, because they follow Jesus Christ who showed the way. Christian prophetic action is borne on prayer that cries not for political victory so much as for the spread of sincere understanding of opponents who so torment us with their accusations and whom we irritate with our indictments.

Empathy yields insight into our enemies's motivations and convictions that may actually lead to more effective strategies for social action. But fundamentally empathy operates in a way that is perpendicular to the ordinary logic of power and control in human relationships. Empathy unites us with our enemies. We are all people in need of love and security, acceptance and understanding. We are often afraid and insecure, and so we formulate brash statements of exclusion that calm our fears and make us feel more at home. Meanwhile, we bond with those who are like us because they accept us as we are and do not challenge us to rethink the basis of our moral judgments and religious feelings.

But Jesus's message, like Paul's, is different. They preached that feeling the pain and joy of the Other, caring for the Other, and sacrificing ourselves for the Other, though it makes no sense by the standards of this world's wisdom, is precisely the foolishness of the cross that can make all the difference. Jesus said "Love your enemies" (Matt. 5:44, Luke 6:27, 35) and lived as though he meant it.

LOVE

Paul consummates his meditation on the body of Christ with the hymn to love in 1 Corinthians 13. "If I speak in the tongues of mortals and of angels, but do not have love, I am a noisy gong or a clanging cymbal" (1 Cor. 13:1). The sociological-moral principles of flocking, perseverance, humility, and empathy culminate in the principle of love.

We don't need an immense amount of life experience to recognize how important love is. We all long for it. We are transformed when we find it and also when we give it. We agonize over the lack of it in our own lives. We wither when we can find no love within us for others. It is not surprising, therefore, that almost all religious traditions make a big deal out of love. Christianity emphasizes love in a particularly strong way because of its Christ-centeredness.

The path of love was the story of Jesus's life, as the early Christian witnesses describe his teaching and ministry. For him, love opened up into healing, justice, and fellowship with God. The same is true for us. Embodying these virtues and bearing such fruits is what it means to follow Jesus as the Christ, as Lord and Savior, as Healer and Example. Love defeats clever calculations of social probabilities, bubbles up where it is not expected, and changes human hearts more quickly and surely than any doctrine.

These unpredictabilities of love are marks of the divine Spirit's presence in the world. They make it difficult to organize an institution around the principle of love. Love is not controlled by institutions, even those that promote it. Rather, love sees across boundaries, looks right through social structures, and joyfully neglects proprieties of class and culture in the name of an egalitarian vision of creative transformation.

Love, of course, is not just one thing. In fact, perseverance, humility, and empathy are all important parts of love, so love is multifaceted in every context. But love also has different qualities in different contexts. Many theologians have pointed out the different words for love in the Greek language of the New Testament. *Eros* is a bodily, sensual connection that answers the longings of our animal nature and helps us to bond in a way that stabilizes communities and creates healthy homes for our children. *Philia* is the love of friendship that gives us the strength of knowing that we are accepted as we are, that draws us outward into confident exploration of our social and natural environments, and that binds our efforts into civilization-building projects. *Storge* is the love of natural affection between friends and family members. *Xenia* is the love of courteous hospitality and concern for friend and stranger alike. *Agape* is the untamed and irrepressible empathic regard of the Other in all its forms, even the hostile enemy and the incomprehensible alien.

Agape has the strength of the Earth and the mercurial character of the butterfly. It cuts across our aspirations and our schemes, calls us far beyond our best strengths and our worst insecurities, and most deeply satisfies us even while promising no worldly success or recognition. To follow Jesus Christ is to embrace this love, not as the rule of life for it cannot be so channeled, but as the gift we give to others because we received it first out of the hand of God. It is the power of *agape* that makes church unity possible in the face of pluralism—even when it flies against the sociological odds.

One of our friends puts it this way. "If you look around at the pews and see some you would never normally spend time with, then you know that is Jesus bringing you together. If that is not happening, then you are just in a Christian country club. And I am absolutely uninterested in devoting my life to that."

CHAPTER 9

Living with Imperfection: Church Splits and the Ecumenical Ideal

In the previous chapter, we sketched a classic solution to the problem of Christian pluralism, one with historic credentials and genuine practical value in contemporary cultural contexts. The recipe is stern but simple: we flock as we will, but then we persevere in a community, cultivate humility and empathy in the face of differences, and above all manifest love in all our dealings with one another. But surely only a fool could believe that love will keep us together under all circumstances. Are not the differences too pronounced, the tendency to flock too strong, the fear of the Other too overpowering, and the human obsession with purity too great?

Our friend Florence is a young pastor serving a congregation with a very experienced senior minister. She told us about her senior colleague's policy on disagreements. "We can't talk about controversial issues in our church without fighting, so we just don't talk about them at all," he explains. Florence can see the hard-earned wisdom in this viewpoint but has a difficult time accepting that the church has to rest content with a don't-ask-don't-tell policy for theological and political disagreements. She wants the church to achieve a deeper and more authentic interaction among Christians.

REALITY OF CHURCH SPLITTING

Sadly, the history of the church, not to mention world history, shows with brutal clarity how quickly human beings fall into wars and divisions, how rapidly we sacrifice love on the altar of security and comfort. Severe pluralism might not defeat the unifying power of love in theory, but in practice it has broken the church over and over again. Splitting the church is an extreme strategy for dealing with the problem of pluralism. It is a solution to pluralism in the way that amputation is a kind of medical treatment. It might be necessary for optimizing health but it is still a disaster for an institution that calls itself "the body of Christ."

The first deep church split, between the Judaizing party and the party of Paul and Peter and James, was agonizing for all concerned. At stake was whether Christianity had to remain culturally Jewish and whether it was right to spread a Jewish rabbi's teachings to ritually impure Gentiles (non-Jews). There were clear and opposed answers, each with impressive theological rationales. But violence took over and the ideological split cut so deeply that unity became impossible. Luke's account of the Jerusalem Conference (Acts 15:1–35) presents the key moment of decision, which unfolded at a time when the vast majority of people involved in the Christian movement, and all of the key decision makers, were Jewish.

Understandably, Acts relates the story from the perspective of the eventual victors. Reading between the lines we can imagine how betrayed the losers must have felt. In the name of empathy, let us picture their point of view. They must have believed that Jesus would have wept over the church's decision to stop being an exclusively Jewish movement. They must have been deeply worried that their wayward brothers and sisters were falling prey to an arrogant belief, namely, that Paul's way had to be the only way for all people regardless of cultural heritage. The Judaizers were not only defending a Jewish way of life; they were resisting an ugly kind of absolutism that pretended that God works in one and only one channel in the world. Paul's party was embracing compromise of Jesus's religion for the sake of wider cultural acceptance and a universal, exclusive message.

For Jewish Christians, the Jewish community was precious, full of neighbors and friends. That is where the Christians belonged, with those who loved them, who understood them. But a Christian Jew who met with Christian Gentiles during the week was ritually impure and unable to attend synagogue on the Sabbath with fellow Jews. The issue of admitting Gentiles to the church was shredding the very fabric of the Jewish community. So it was a terrible fight, not only about the meaning of the gospel but also about the meaning of being God's chosen people. It took several decades for the battle to subside, as Paul's ongoing violent encounters with the Judaizing party attest. In fact, it only really began to end when Gentile Christians vastly outnumbered Jewish Christians, which made the intra-Jewish debate more or less beside the point. And it only truly ended when the Romans destroyed the Jerusalem temple in 70 CE, reducing Judaism to a series of small communities scattered across the empire. Before it ended, however, it was extremely ugly and dangerous, and is what triggered the split inaugurated by the Jerusalem Council.

Historically, church splits helped manage national and cultural differences, and accommodated stubborn church leaders, without falling into war. The Catholic Church did not need to stand by and watch King Henry VIII split off the English Church from the rest. They could have gone to war against England, even as the English themselves fought bitterly over how to run their new church (was it Catholic or Protestant or something else?). Indeed, it still fights over this, albeit less violently. But the split occurred without massive violence between Continental and English Catholics. Not enough boats perhaps.

The Catholic Church ejected Martin Luther, and thousands of churches all over Europe followed the Reformers, partly as a way of coping with a vast and deep spiritual and theological split within the church. There was terrible violence and torture but rarely did it erupt into all-consuming war because entire towns tended to follow the opinion of the wealthy noblemen who were their benefactors and protectors.

The Anglican Church was distinctly inhospitable to John Wesley, whose Methodist movement swept like wildfire through the English and North American working classes, changing lives wherever it went. But the Methodists eventually met in new churches where the new people didn't make the existing church folk feel uncomfortable. So violence was largely avoided.

Mainline Protestants found it much easier to deal with their Pentecostal brethren when the Pentecostals met in their own churches. The Pentecostals felt the same way, so a massive movement grew all over the world parallel to, and largely separate from, mainline Protestantism. And all this occurred without devastating violence.

Clearly there is good evidence for the peace-preserving effects of church splits. This alone makes church splitting a valuable way to cope with pluralism when the classic and ideal solution fails. It follows that "church splitting" is a required category for making sociological sense of the history of Christianity. The social dynamics of church splits seem fairly clear. We can all probably agree that splits are inevitable, at least sometimes, from a sociological point of view. But when we move from describing to evaluating the situation, we quickly run into problems.

THEOLOGY OF CHURCH SPLITTING

The theological status of church splitting is a deeply divided question. On the one hand, theologians may believe that the church is authentically present on both sides of a split, before and after it occurs. That is, theologically speaking, a split is a *division*. In this case, church splits are not theologically inspired solutions to pluralism. They are circumstantial, last-resort ways of coping with pluralism and disagreement when the stress of difference just becomes too much to handle. Splits express genuine disagreement, and they represent failure of the principles of perseverance, humility, empathy, and love in the face of the relentless power of the flocking principle and our own ever-present weakness and insecurity. Such theologians would hesitate to include in their ecclesiology books a chapter on the theological justification of brutal and painful church divisions, even if such divisions do serve to keep the peace.

On the other hand, theologians may believe that the church was impure prior to a split and that the true church is only on one side of the split afterwards. That is, theologically speaking, a split is a *separation.* In this case, church splits are theologically mandated solutions to the problems of apostasy and heresy. The pure church either discharges its impure portions and heretical elements, or it leaves the apostate church in order to preserve a faithful remnant. This remnant is the authentic body of Christ, on this view, so no harm is done to that Body when separation occurs; rather, the Body is protected. Splits are not amputations that remove a natural part of the body, but operations that remove an unnatural cancerous growth. On this view, peace and unity are less important than purity of doctrine and practice.

Division and separation are decidedly different theological attitudes toward church splits. Sometimes they co-exist. In the heat of the moment, the leaders of both sides of a church split probably believe that a separation is needed for the sake of purifying the church and purging it of moral and theological sickness. They just disagree over which parts are pure and which are defiled. Later, perhaps many centuries later, ecumenical instincts can lead to rapprochement, with leaders on both sides speaking of the split as an unfortunate division that should be reversed or at least regretted.

We are all familiar with the value of a cooling-off period when an argument gets too hot to handle. Church institutions don't plan cooling-off periods but they occur nonetheless, and they can be very long indeed. For example, it was only around Vatican II (1962–1965) that the Roman Catholic Church was able officially to recognize some authenticity in the churches of the Reformation. That is a cooling-off period of over four centuries. Much the same was true for the Protestant side.

Of course, individual people and parts of institutions cool at different rates. So it is not difficult to find scattered examples of cooperation and dialogue between Protestants and Roman

Catholics. Nor is it difficult to find conservative elements on both sides for whom regret over the Reformation split is unthinkable. Some Roman Catholics regard Vatican II and its sponsor, Pope John XXIII, as expressing the very height of Catholic apostasy and heresy because of its accommodating attitudes to Protestants, Jews, world religions, modern scholarship, and contemporary culture. Likewise, some Protestants still regale their young people with stories of the horrible tortures inflicted by Catholics on the Protestant faithful centuries ago and would be absolutely horrified if one of their children wanted to marry a Catholic.

We believe a realistic theology of the church will recognize the sociological role of church splits. But the fact that some people think of such splits as purifying separations does not make them so unambiguously. Church splitting is not a clear-cut question of *either* division *or* separation. On the contrary, there is authenticity and wickedness in all human institutions, including the church. A church can become more corrupt with time, and it can also become more faithful. Most churches continually undergo transformations in both directions at once in different places and in various ways. This fact of human life shows that self-congratulatory identifications of one's group as the "pure remnant" of the church are self-deceptive, just as arrogant dismissals of vast sections of Christianity as "apostate and heretical" are pitifully self-serving.

BALANCING PURITY AND UNITY

We are ecumenically minded and resolutely opposed to the nurturing of hatred toward the Other in all its forms. Yet we have argued that harmony and tolerance are not overriding values. Sometimes we need to fight for what we believe and not tolerate the evil we see around us, even in the church. Sometimes we must refuse to give what is holy to dogs (Matt. 7:6), even in the church. But ambiguity is a fact of life so it is vital that we humbly acknowledge weakness and failure in our own lives and our own institutions as least as clearly as in the lives and institutions of others. We must observe Jesus's injunction not to judge, for we are creatures who can easily notice a speck in our neighbor's eye while overlooking a log in our own (Matt. 7:1–5).

The proximity of the last two cited passages in Matthew's presentation of the Sermon on the Mount is thought provoking. One says do not judge so that you may not be judged, while the other presumes that we need to judge others at times, as dogs unfit for holy things, no less. This expresses our situation perfectly. We need to judge, yes, and yet, such is the moral danger in judging others that we need to judge ourselves with at least as much perceptiveness and determination.

From our point of view, then, church splits are never ideal even when they are practically unavoidable and useful. By contrast with the tension-easing convenience of church splits, the classic solution to pluralism we have sketched—perseverance, humility, empathy, and love—tries to hold people together despite the tension of difference. This was Paul's vision of the church, at least as the church should be ideally. Jesus seems to have thought much this way about his little band of followers, judging from his command that they should love one another (see especially John 14–17). Both groups were decidedly minority communities under fire, which makes maintaining unity vital. Nevertheless, even when the church is part of the majority culture, we need to respect this ideal and try to live up to it. When we cannot maintain the ideal of unity, we should regard church splits with regret rather than indulge our self-righteous impulse to gloat over authentic remnants, thereby assigning ourselves the moral high ground, from which we invite the harsher judgment.

Can there be a successful church split? We think so, in a sense. The first major split certainly proved to be historically decisive and the violence and hatred around it did eventually abate. But it also laid the groundwork for an appalling history of Christian anti-Semitism. So it was successful in some senses even if it also had evil and tragic side effects that were incalculable at the time.

Was the split within the Methodist Episcopal Church over slavery successful? The denomination was officially opposed to slavery, following the opinion of its founder, John Wesley, but many southern Methodists owned slaves. A controversy over this issue led the southern part of the church to withdraw in 1844, founding the Methodist Episcopal Church, South. After the Civil War a couple of decades later, almost all African Americans left the Methodist Episcopal Church, South for the northern Methodist church or for denominations of their own. Despite the tragedy of the split, it prevented fighting, allowed the southern church to remain continuous with its social environment's support of slavery, and also allowed the northern church to maintain a more consistent prophetic stance against slavery. Moreover, with the slavery issue settled in the Civil War, the two parts eventually reunited in 1939, along with other denominations, repairing the damage. Perhaps the long-view conclusion would have to be that this, too, was a successful church split.

Are church splits sometimes necessary? We think so. In relation to the original church split, tolerating deep disagreement about whether Christianity could extend beyond Judaism is virtually impossible to conceive. Much the same is true of other debated points in famous church splits, including the Methodist split just recounted. We conclude that ecclesiology must have a place for church splits. They can be done in different ways, of course. As in all things, the loving way is best.

Can there be loving church splits? We think so. Rather than invoking one-sided categories such as "purification of the true church" or "withdrawal of the faithful remnant" to explain theologically what is going on in a church split, we think that categories such as "irreconcilable disagreement" and "parting of the ways" are theologically superior. The good and the true and the beautiful are on both sides of every church split—ambiguously and impurely. Extremists may believe that the "pure church" is on only one side, but there are such fanatical elements on both sides. Later generations see this clearly, often with remorse.

The ecclesiological analysis of church splits should keep love in first place, always, and humbly recognize that, even when splitting is unavoidable, it is not ideal. And when splits happen, those involved can aim to be as loving as possible and to minimize harm to the body of Christ.

Implementing the Ecumenical Ideal

The ecumenical vision we have laid out powerfully encourages unity and is also realistic about the inevitability of church splits. It offers a biblically informed theological interpretation of both staying together and falling apart. But how do we implement it in practice? Is not unity too easily overcome by conflict and dissention? How do we realize any ideal of Christian unity when liberals and evangelicals are at each other's throats within every major Protestant denomination, with each one seemingly ready to split over contentious theological and moral issues? We need to think further about implementation on the large scale as well as on the local and personal levels.

Implementation on the Large Scale

The problem with large scale implementation is painfully obvious. Despite the best efforts of the ecumenical movement, there are a lot of different churches out there. Some individual congregations here and there approximate this ideal of unity—we have seen such congregations all over the world, from small New England towns to Atlanta suburbs to inner city Los Angeles communities, in England and Germany, in Australia and South Africa, in China and India. But the ideal of unity certainly is not working in the church as a whole. It is under threat in the worldwide Anglican Communion and in a number of mainline denominations in many countries.

How can a denomination hold together over divisive issues such as gay marriage or abortion? How can a single denomination contain the theological and political diversity of fundamentalists, conservatives, evangelicals, neo-evangelicals, liberals, and progressives? Do we surrender Paul's ecclesial vision when social and political realities press hard upon us? Do we give up the Christian ideal of unity in Christ and split churches over every major moral issue? God knows that the banner of Christian unity lies in tatters and covered in mud beneath the warring divisions of post-Reformation Christianity.

The ideal of Christian unity seems hopelessly idealistic on the large scale. The Christian understanding of church promises a different kind of community, one with a higher standard of unity than that of human groups beyond the borders of the church, a greater capacity for diversity, and a tougher command of love. But the hard fact is that churches cannot tolerate a lot of pluralism and diversity, not even as much as most secular institutions—togetherness is more challenging in the presence of longings for intimacy and like-mindedness.

We tell ourselves the church should decide to split as a last resort, as a concession to hardness of hearts rather than as a way to avoid discomfort with differently minded brothers and sisters (the way Mark 10:2–9 recalls Jesus's interpretation of Moses's teaching on divorce might be pertinent here). But the church has split quickly often enough—more quickly and more often than nations and major secular institutions in the last five centuries—and there is profound hostility among warring branches of the church. Extreme true believers would not even accept the phrase "branches of the church" because it suggests a tree (perhaps the apostle Paul's olive tree in Romans 11:16–24) with each branch a proper part of the tree, whereas they believe theirs is the only true church. Implementing the classic solution to pluralism in the church seems impossible on the large scale.

Implementation on the Local Scale

At the root of the large-scale implementation problem we have just sketched, and also at the root of North American culture wars, is the pluralism of local differences. What is not reconciled locally cannot be harmonized nationally or culturally, not even in churches. So it is in local congregations that we discover how serious we are about Christian love. This should not be surprising. Local churches and communities, neighborhoods and families are the places where most Christians have a great deal at stake. They care deeply about their local churches and most are more willing to fight over what they know and need locally than over abstract issues of denominational identity. It is at the local level that church unity first breaks down under the pressure of theological and spiritual diversity and it is also at the local level where the small and large triumphs of unity in love most often occur.

Local pastors know this all too well. Most have had experiences both of wondrous togetherness and of intractable disagreements in churches. They have seen forgiveness and resentful fights that never end even when many aspects of a congregation's corporate life are going well. They have seen people leave while others stay and fight. Sometimes these fights are about turf battles or personality conflicts or sociopathic behavior, all of which have little real importance beyond the harm they cause. But substantive issues are often at stake in local church fights: what to believe in doctrine and morals, how to conduct worship, or the appropriateness of spiritual practices. Church fights over the Vietnam War affected most congregations in the countries that sent troops. American churches have fought over the placement of the U.S. flag, how much money to give to mission projects, and the style of preaching and worship in their congregation.

Conflicting authentic interpretations of Christianity—what we have been calling "core-message pluralism"—drive theological and moral diversity within local congregations. There is not one right way to be a church, judging from church history. There is no incontestable or unambiguous formulation of doctrine, judging from the history of theology. There are no moral laws that win assent regardless of context, judging from the history of ethics. There are no spiritual practices that are static and timeless, judging from the history of spirituality and worship. As a result, there is not a single obvious way to be judged authentically Christian.

Extremists will disagree, but then their extremism forces them into a posture of special pleading on behalf of their "true variant" as it allegedly threads its way through the much larger and richer history of what they must think of as the "generally apostate" Christian churches. True believers of this sort should read another book. We take the core-message pluralism of authentic Christianity seriously. It is this pluralism that makes important church disagreements not always a matter of right versus wrong but sometimes one right versus another right. This is the nature of the local implementation problem facing the classic vision of Christian unity.

Implementation at the Personal Level

The personal implementation problem has to do with how each individual makes up his or her mind about what being a Christian means and how we then deal with people who have come to different decisions. If there were no pluralism of authentic Christianity, then making up our minds about what it means to be a Christian would be easy. Unfortunately—or fortunately, as we see things—it is not easy. It is not easy even in groups that censor information about Christian diversity to protect their young people's faith development—and a glance over church school curricula shows that most Christian groups indulge such censorship to various degrees.

In fact, becoming Christian in a faithful way can be exquisitely painful, a process filled with doubt and misgivings, and dogged by keen awareness that there are other people we want to love and respect who do not believe as we do. It is further clouded by generic knowledge of psychological and social processes of projection and self-deception. With time and maturity, the art of being a distinctive person with specific beliefs while still acknowledging authenticity in other faithful Christians and good non-Christians becomes easier to master. But the journey can be a harrowing one.

Most seminary students understand the personal challenge of claiming one's faith authentically and wholeheartedly in the face of pluralism of authentic expressions of Christianity. As the "seminary journey" story at the beginning of chapter 1 expresses, students arrive in seminary formed in their local congregational cultures and usually by a university education. They have already fought many personal battles about who they will be, what they will believe, and how they will live, in the face of some awareness of the world's religious pluralism and the diversity of forms of life in their own society. Despite warnings, seminary education opens up another kind of pluralism, namely, pluralism of belief and practice within Christianity itself.

For some students, church history may be the hardest class because it makes the record of Christian diversity and conflict so obvious. For others, it may be the introduction to theology or the introduction to ethics. For yet others it may be introductory Bible courses, where they encounter modes of interpretation that appreciate the Scriptures while not hesitating to ask difficult textual, historical, moral, and theological questions. For most seminary students, the challenge is how to take seriously the diversity of Christianity in history, belief, and practice while forging a stable and spiritually potent identity as a Christian leader.

If seminary students successfully run this gauntlet at the beginning of their theological education, they begin to reforge their identity in a more robust and refined way. This can be surprising to them but it is enormously rewarding. It turns out that they did not need the old patterns of comfort and security as much as they had initially thought. They can commit themselves to a more complex mission in a more ambiguous world and feel confident in their faith as they do so. They can resolve to be a committed Christian even though they know other committed Christians disagree with their theology and politics, and they can do this with maturity and compassion that was unimaginable before they started out on the journey.

One of our colleagues, Paul, relates a story from his seminary days. After a semester of tough survey courses, one of Paul's friends felt completely disoriented and complained, "Man, they're trying to steal my Jesus." Paul recalls sympathizing with the spiritual stress at discovering a world of Christianity that was so different from that of his local church. But Paul also felt that gaining this new knowledge caused scales to fall from his eyes. He puts it this way: "I *knew* there was something the church wasn't telling me!" Paul asked his local pastor why the church did not share the wonderful knowledge of the complex history and theology of Christianity with ordinary Christians. His pastor replied, "They're not ready." Paul was not so sure. But he was sure that the transformation in his perspective made his faith far more robust and strengthened his leadership abilities.

Another colleague, Jenny, just doesn't buy the often-repeated complaint that learning about core-message pluralism destroys faith. It didn't work that way for her. When she was in college she read the Bible from cover to cover because God was at the center of her life. But it didn't mean much to her at the time. It wasn't until seminary that the Bible really came alive for Jenny. Her education in the complexities of biblical interpretation and the history of Christianity was crucial for her to gain deep satisfaction from her Bible reading.

Implementation of the ecumenical idea at the large-scale level of the entire church seems impossible. At the local level, implementation is the great challenge that all church congregations have to face. It is particularly important in liberal-evangelical congregations that make a deliberate attempt to cultivate a significant and uncomfortable degree of pluralism. The personal level is where implementing the ecumenical ideal is most under our control, but not everyone is interested in making this kind of love real in their lives. For those Christians with the courage to undertake the ecumenical journey within their own lives, however, it is a hugely satisfying process. And that's why they keep searching for liberal-evangelical churches that practice Christ-centered radical inclusivism and proclaim a clear gospel message.

A Moderate Conclusion

If you are a Christian moderate of the liberal-evangelical kind, you are probably deeply inspired by Jesus's vision for the unity of his followers (John 14–17). You are invested in Paul's idea of Christian unity (perseverance, humility, empathy, love). You believe these ideals ought to apply to keeping moderate liberals and moderate evangelicals together in local congregations. The idea of Republicans and Democrats worshiping side by side excites and comforts you. The vision of pro-life and pro-choice moderates teaching church school together intrigues you. You are personally committed to working for unity across ideological and theological differences as testimony to the power of love. You long for a church that will commit itself to that vision. Most likely you do not currently belong to such a church but you feel that you would give yourself wholeheartedly to that kind of congregational mission.

Many moderates have given up on serious Christian unity on scales larger than local congregations. They celebrate the many wonderful examples of cooperation within and between denominations, from denomination-based mission efforts to local minister's ecumenical organizations. But they recognize that efforts to unite denominations into new denominations cannot succeed except in the limited sense that massive numerical contraction and aging membership make denominational unity necessary. This kind of unity is more like huddling around the last fire on a cold winter night than a testimony to divine love that comprehends and transcends difference. Yet they have strong hopes that congregations can demonstrate unity that goes against the cultural grain and defies sociological probabilities.

We think the greatest hope for implementing a countercultural vision of Christian unity is through lay and ordained church leaders, including seminary students. The reframing of identity we are describing can be the lesson of their lives. It can perpetually reassure them in the face of subsequent conflict that perseverance pays off, that humility and gratitude keep opponents together, that empathy brings understanding where negotiation alone cannot, and that love can forge unity in the face of the deepest and most authentic disagreements. These are the people who can lead the liberal-evangelical congregations that will become places for moderate Christians to discover and manifest the divine love that transcends cultural and political differences.

Were such congregations to become more numerous, the aspirations of Protestant denominations to hold together despite internal diversity would change from being futile pipe dreams to potentially viable political strategies. In the meantime, each liberal-evangelical congregation is a precious island of hope for moderates, and a place where they can feel truly at home.

PART IV

The Radical Moderate

CHAPTER 10

Radical Discipleship for Moderate Christians

In this chapter and the next two, we explicitly take up the practical question of how discerning moderate Christians should live, focusing on three issues. We first address the sense in which discerning Christian moderates are committed to a radical form of Christian discipleship, and spell out what that means for everyday life. In the following chapter, we take up practical questions facing churches that are determined to exhibit both Christ-centeredness and radical inclusiveness in their corporate life. Finally, we address the radically countercultural character of Christian ethics from a moderate perspective. We conclude part IV with a meditation on the paradox of "radical moderates."

As we ponder the ethics of moderate Christians of the liberal and evangelical kind, we can't help thinking of the words of a pop hit from the 1970s. Being stuck in the middle may be the best possible place we can be.

> Yes I'm stuck in the middle with you
> And I'm wondering what it is I should do
> It's so hard to keep the smile from my face
> Losing control, yeah I'm all over the place
> Clowns to the left of me, jokers to the right
> Here I am, stuck in the middle with you.
> —Gerry Rafferty, "Stuck In the Middle with You," 1973

What's Radical about Christian Discipleship?

Let's begin this exploration of the radical quality of Christian discipleship as moderates conceive it by reflecting on a couple of Bible passages that have been vital to the church's interpretation of discipleship over the centuries.

> As Jesus and his disciples were on their way, he came to a village where a woman named Martha opened her home to him. She had a sister called Mary, who sat at the Lord's feet listening to what he said...Martha came to him and asked, "Lord don't you care that my sister has left me to do the work by myself? Tell her to help me!" "Martha, Martha," the Lord answered, "you are worried and upset about many things, but only one thing is needed. Mary has chosen what is better, and it will not be taken away from her." (Luke 10:38–42 NIV)

> As Jesus started on his way, a man ran up to him and fell on his knees before him. "Good teacher," he asked, "what must I do to inherit eternal life?"... Jesus looked at him and loved him. "One thing you lack," he said. "Go, sell everything you have and give to the poor, and you will have treasure in heaven. Then come, follow me." (Mark 10:17–21 NIV)

These two gospel passages convey two sides of the meaning of radical Christian discipleship. The first is about placing Jesus Christ at the center of life, and the second is about changing life priorities to express the centrality of Christ. It is easy to imagine why followers of Jesus Christ in the generations between the birth of the church and the widespread sharing of the gospel writings preserved these stories. It would have been extremely important to them to tell each other about the way Jesus encouraged those who wanted to follow him to love him completely and to live for him devotedly. It would have been especially important to focus on stories like that at times when Christians were persecuted for their faith.

What do Christ-centeredness and lifestyle transformation mean for discerning moderate Christians in our place and time?

There is not a single answer to this question because our complex cultures support a staggering array of lifestyles. This makes discerning a faithful Christian lifestyle a truly difficult challenge.

Christ-centeredness

Whole-hearted spirituality requires focus. The world and our lives are awash in busy activity. On any given day there are a thousand distractions that can draw us away from our sacred center. We choose soccer over Sabbath. We choose work over worship. We choose play dates over prayer. We find our lives governed more by "Just Do It" and "Grab, Gulp, and Go" advertising campaigns than by the gospel. We easily lose track of our calling to love God and neighbor. Like Martha's busy caring, our busy and useful lives can obscure the "one thing" that is most essential in life, attention to God and God's call on our lives.

How are we to maintain focus in a culture stuffed full of advertising, stress, and activity? For those traveling in the Christian way, Jesus Christ is the model for focusing on God. In becoming a disciple of Christ, in following Christ every day, in placing Christ at the center of life, we learn to focus on God. Some folks like to deal with God without thinking too much about Jesus Christ, and we will not object. But in Jesus Christ, Christians have an example and a teacher, a companion and an inspiring guide. Like Mary, Christians can learn to keep their eyes on Jesus. They can sit at his feet by reading the portrayals of him in the gospels.

Jesus was an actual human presence for Martha and Mary. They could focus on Jesus if they chose to in the most natural of ways. Mary could temporarily set aside her housework obligations to sit with Jesus, listen to his words, and keep her eyes on him. For Christians reading this story and longing to do the same, things are very different. Everyone has the biblical pictures of Jesus, which are invaluable even though they are sometimes difficult to understand and require careful study. The Christian tradition is replete with spiritual meditations on Jesus Christ, scholarly studies of the gospel accounts of his life, and theological reflections on his religious significance. For some, there are spiritual experiences of encounter with the living Christ, perhaps in prayer or mediated through the Eucharist or the Christian community. For others, there is the imaginative picturing of how Jesus would advise them or how he would behave in a particular situation (what would Jesus do?). Contemporary Christians do not have what Mary had and may wistfully long for it. But they have rich resources to help them be consistently Christ-centered, providing they know where those resources are and how to make good use of them.

Moderate Christians of the liberal and evangelical type always seek to keep Jesus Christ at the center of their lives, while earnestly striving to include all of their sisters and brothers in their fellowship. This is a constant challenge because the moment Christians decide to place Christ at the center of their lives or churches, they are forced to look at Christ's life and teachings more closely. In doing so, the always forceful and sometimes sacrificial character of Christ's message can draw us into areas of genuine discomfort. Jesus had strong convictions. He said that love of God and love of neighbor come first. Homeland security, manifest destiny, and proclaiming a gospel of prosperity are not mentioned.

Liberal-evangelical moderates are committed to following Christ even when discipleship gets hard. They read the gospel in context, which makes biblical interpretation both more complex and more convincing. They understand that they will have only arrived when they find themselves standing at the back of the line. They believe that in weakness God's power is most fully revealed. They understand freedom is not free, but they are more willing to pay the even higher cost of peace. They believe the gospel is not the path to easy street, but the path that takes us to those who live on the streets.

Needless to say, this is a message the world at large does not preach. In fact, it is a radical message that most televangelists and megachurch pastors refuse to preach because it destroys the culturally compromised forms of Christianity that they prefer. Nor is it often heard from mainline church pulpits, whose own form of culture Christianity would be disrupted by the topsy-turvy view of the world that Jesus Christ proclaims. The only way Christians will ever be able to keep to the path Jesus Christ sets out for them is if they follow in his footsteps and never take their eyes from his witness and example. Radical Christian discipleship means making Jesus Christ central to life. Nothing else and no one else will do.

Christ-centered Lifestyles

Living a Christ-centered life takes discipline and determination. Christians of all sorts, and indeed people of all faiths, are daily assaulted by a complex culture of delights that tempts us to "follow our bliss" instead of discerning our ultimate destiny. If they are sufficiently determined, then they will sell what they have to, quit what they have to, and do whatever they have to so that they can follow Jesus Christ. That is the point of Mark's story about the man whom Jesus instructs to give all he has to the poor and follow him. Radical discipleship for followers of Christ can involve surprising lifestyle choices. How should moderate Christians who are determined to live Christ-centered lives think through their lifestyle choices?

For the sake of specificity, we will focus on money. While the Bible has many diverse teachings about money, Jesus's teaching is quite consistent. Luke presents Jesus's most important parable about money in Luke 16:1–13, which concludes with a famous line: "You cannot serve God and mammon" (13 NKJV). Is money mammon from hell, as Jesus and Luke suggest? Or is it manna from heaven, the key to health and happiness and a form of divine blessing? Jesus's perspective on money, wealth, poverty, and economic justice is painfully out of sync with our way of life. Jesus and Luke never remotely imagined our economic circumstances. Yet there is something timeless about the Bible's and Jesus's preference for the poor and marginalized. So how should we think about money and what should we do to make our lifestyles conform with Jesus's vision of justice?

One of us recalls just beginning to lead a Sunday evening worship service when a young woman entered the door of the church with a child about six years old. They both looked unhealthy. The woman was strung out on drugs and desperate for money. The child may have been the woman's daughter or just borrowed for effect. The congregation was confused because of the awkward timing, but she was given enough money for a couple of meals and referred to local shelters and programs that doubtless she already knew full well. This was a heartbreaking scene of desperate need and child abuse, scenes common around that church. Most people feel compassion joined with a shudder of horror when they contemplate such a desperate situation. The driving principle of Jesus's view of money is as simple and direct as those emotions of compassion and horror. The Hebrew Bible and Jesus's teaching alike prioritize the poor and vulnerable, the sick and lonely, the marginalized and disenfranchised. Economic arrangements that protect and support those people are good. Economic arrangements that do not are wicked. It is an uncompromising litmus test. At no point does the Bible apologize for being idealistic and compassionate in its litmus test for economic justice.

The most loudly trumpeted Christian view of money at the current time is the prosperity gospel. Just as God took care of the Israelites in the desert with manna from heaven, so God will send you money, in proportion to your faith and generosity. This is routinely used as a fundraising technique on radio and television religious broadcasts and there is no shortage of books to fill in the details, in case you are wondering how to get in on this remarkable financial scheme. This popular Christian view has some biblical support, but not in Jesus's teachings about money. It reminds us of New Guinea cargo cults. Our Bible-translating missionary friends used to tell us about native people going into a dangerous frenzy every time an airplane arrived from the sky gods with wondrous goods and supplies. If they could get their religious rituals just right, they believed, they could induce the gods to send more planes with more good stuff. The similarity with the prosperity gospel is palpable. If we live and believe just right, we can get God mysteriously to send us all this good stuff.

We all know how hardworking and imaginative people get their money, and God does not send it from heaven. Religion sometimes helps people be hardworking and imaginative but powerful economic systems that create good jobs and opportunities matter more. Being the most prosperous nation on earth conveys deadly serious responsibilities and brings not divine blessing but divine judgment.

Everywhere we look, it seems, Jesus's view of money and wealth is ignored. But his teaching does not budge: money is manna from heaven when used to support the poor and defenseless but its influence on our moral sense and our social priorities can make it mammon from hell. We may be able to admit this, despite its uncomfortable implications for seeking to live out radical lifestyles of Christ-centered discipleship. Yet something seems missing.

In Jesus's context, wealth was rare and brought great power. It meant profiting from a system that kept most people hard underfoot. That's how it goes in economies with no middle class and not much of a social welfare system, both in ancient times and today. It is no wonder that Jesus's pro-peasant preaching insisted that you can't serve God and money. But what would Jesus or Luke say about flexible economies full of opportunities for creative and disciplined people? What would they say about subtle adjustments in a Federal Reserve interest rate, tuning economic growth to create employment while keeping inflation in check? Or about international loans used to leverage social and economic change in poor nations? Or about the way global free trade spreads wealth but also brings hated economic and cultural side-effects?

Our world is not the world of the New Testament and it is not easy to apply Jesus's and Luke's views of money to our economic lifestyle choices. Whereas Luke calls money unrighteous, we give our children weekly pocket money to help them learn how to manage money, partly because we have seen how economic activity can be a means of personal growth. Should we teach our kids that money is evil instead? We have seen wise economic support gradually transform run-down communities, improving health and welfare for thousands, as well as the reverse process due to economic neglect. Should we reject the prosperity and safety brought by wealth and productivity as wrongheaded?

Jesus was a great advocate of the poor. But how do we follow his example? Does caring for the poverty-stricken mean tax-funded social welfare programs or do we replace government help with a thousand nonprofit points of compassionate light? Most people by now have heard about microloans to the poor, initiated by Muhammad Yunus's amazing Grameen Bank in Bangladesh. But the Hebrew Bible and the Qur'an both ban interest on loans for people within their own communities, a policy that would destroy microloan initiatives. Does caring for the poor allow us to ignore these sacred texts on this question and spread microloans around the world?

Unfortunately, Jesus did not talk much about the economic arrangements of his own time, which might have helped us figure out how to implement his vision. He did say that his followers should pay taxes to the Roman Empire that occupied their country; they were Caesar's coins, after all. But that is a tough sell for Americans who revolted over taxation by a foreign government. Jewish law dictated a schedule of debt forgiveness but debt holders routinely preserved loans by transferring them to holding companies when debt relief time came. Did Jesus think this was a sensible way around a silly rule or a devious way to observe the letter of the law while violating its spirit? The most direct financial advice from Jesus preserved in the Bible is what he said to the young man in the passage above. Some saintly people have given away everything and lived with the poor, but they weren't raising families in the United States. We simply do not know how Jesus would advise us to implement his views of money and wealth in his time or in ours.

Let's face it: by global standards, most Americans are wealthy, and on the wrong side of Jesus's teaching on money. But we don't regard our wealth as intrinsically wicked, as unrighteous mammon useful only for buying our way into heaven. We should use our money wisely, to make a difference in the world, to be thankful for the security and comfort that it brings, and to act positively instead of obsessing over money and mortgages and bills and taxes. We need to take a stand against rampant consumption, to be mindful of the whole world and not just our own families, to advocate for global economic responsibility and ecological prudence.

Living a life of poverty in solidarity with the poor might make you one of Jesus's favorites. But if you're not going to do that—and, frankly, we are not—then all we really have to go by is Jesus's litmus test. That is, we can tell how well we are handling the wealth we have by evaluating the circumstances of the poor all around us (see John the Baptist's version of this criterion in Luke 3:7–12). There might be a place in the kingdom of God on Earth for wealth, even though Jesus was poor. There might be room for lovely homes and mortgages, even though Jesus was sometimes homeless. There might even be a role for executives in luxurious boardrooms deciding the fates of thousands of workers, even though Jesus was sometimes unemployed and depended on others for food and shelter. In Jesus's picture of that kingdom, however, there is no place for people who don't care about the vulnerable, who don't acknowledge the effects of their overconsumption, who are numb to the circumstances that immerse children in disease and ignorance and violence, or who refuse to bend their influence to change those circumstances.

Jesus was incredibly idealistic. He didn't care about being economically practical. He wanted us to transform our values, open our eyes to exploitation and poverty, and devote ourselves to God's service. His idealism doesn't make the choices surrounding faithful Christian lifestyles any easier. If they paid attention to it, most church folk today would find Jesus's teaching as offensive as the religious leaders of his own time did. I am sure that most would overhear his message about money and the poor and dismiss it as unrealistic. Yet Jesus would not compromise his idealistic message about money and the poor, not for a second, not even in the smallest degree, not for anyone. Christian discipleship is not called radical for nothing.

How Do Moderate Christians Become Radical Disciples?

The painful truth is that when people get to know what radical Christian discipleship means for their personal outlook on life and for their lifestyle choices, many turn away from the journey. They prefer the comfort of culture-Christianity which, in its various forms, dominates both evangelical and liberal religions.

These are versions of the Christian faith that mute the hard prophetic questions about justice and repress the spiritual goal of Christ-centeredness in the name of enriching material life as we know it. But the strange new world of the Bible disrupts life as we know it.

The more we grasp this strange new world, the more choosing to follow Jesus Christ feels like an alarming all-or-nothing gamble, as it was for those whom Jesus recruited from their fishing jobs beside the Sea of Galilee. They didn't really understand what they were getting themselves into; they just had to choose. We never read about those who said no to Jesus, only the ones that dropped their nets and threw their lot in with him. And then the journey began—a life-changing, mind-bending journey of radical discipleship.

For Christians in our time, there is no personal, face-to-face confrontation with a man with sparkling eyes who boldly asks for our allegiance. For some the journey of Christian discipleship begins with an experience of conversion in which they are born again into a life with new priorities and challenges, and a new community of friends. For others they just find themselves on the path as they grow in devotion to God and learn to center their lives on Jesus Christ as Lord and Example. No matter how it starts, however, the journey of radical discipleship involves many important decisions along the way. It is in these decisions that Christians either become radicalized in their discipleship or else turn their hand from the plough.

The spiritual life is not a destination. It is a sacred pilgrimage whose hallmarks are learning, prayer, and service. All of these have both individual and corporate aspects. They are essential aspects of what Christians traditionally have called sanctification, which is a determined journey in search of integrated holiness in both personal and corporate life. We say a word about each of these three hallmarks.

Learning

Learning in all senses is a crucial factor in grasping the meaning of radical discipleship and learning how to live it out in daily life.

For example, returning to the theme of money, we see that Christian discipleship requires us to learn what the Bible and especially Jesus have to say about money and economic justice, to think it through in relation to our current economic circumstances, and to constantly review the lifestyle decisions we make in light of what we learn. That requires much more than just listening to a stewardship sermon once or twice a year. Discipleship without intensive learning is as inconceivable for contemporary Christians as it was among Jesus's band of followers.

We additionally have a vast cultural chasm to overcome if we are to gain a responsible understanding of the Bible. That takes a lot of homework, from reading the Bible itself to learning about the history and culture of the times through handbooks and commentaries. Learning the original languages has many advantages. But most Christians can do very well by relying on the fabulous resources created by experts who devote their lives to studying the Bible using the very best historical and literary tools. It is especially through careful study that the strange new world of the Bible emerges and is able to affect us by restructuring our imagination and inspiring us to different lifestyle choices.

Many of the decisions we make along the path of Christian discipleship are spurred by new self-awareness due to learning. Because we often unconsciously fall into sinful rhythms of life, a lot turns on what we do when we realize that something is not right. That's why we need regular confession and repentance. We read the story of the rich man and the story of Mary and Martha, not with self-righteous disdain, but with a tender and convicted understanding that we, more often than not, find ourselves in Martha's and the rich man's shoes. Our homes, cars, boats, clothes, jobs, and obligations may be unavoidable but they also threaten to interfere with our devotion. The spiritual life is one of continual course correction with Christ as our guide. We sin, learn, confess, learn, repent, learn, are forgiven, and learn—and then we repeat the cycle again, eager to begin anew. Or perhaps the spiritual life is more akin to cleaning out the barn. The muck piles up, and we clean it out, only for more muck to pile up. We clean and we clean, and we never finish, but we grow in understanding as we shovel out the refuse, and each time we get better at it.

In our weaker moments we imagine ourselves the faithful disciples who leave everything behind to follow Jesus, or we imagine ourselves as Mary seated at the feet of her Lord. That is well and good but these are half-truths at best. A humble and passionate faith contains the twin convictions that we always fall short, but we never stop trying. Like a toddler learning to walk, we expect to fall, but we get up in the hope of learning to stumble less often. This is the peculiar logic of life as a disciple of Jesus Christ.

Confronting our own sin and blind neglect is one of the most spiritually compelling forms of learning. It can bear fruit in the short term and even more in the long term within the framework of a quest for personal holiness. Serving the poor, tending to the sick, and ministering to those in need are not part of our natural survival instincts. We are genetically inclined to look out for our own interests even if it is at the expense of another, and to cooperate only to the extent necessary to further our own interests and the interests of our tribe. Jesus Christ calls us out of our evolutionarily programmed selfishness into a life of service to others. That is such a counterintuitive, countercultural, and even counterbiological move that we need continually to focus on yoking ourselves to the life and teachings of Jesus Christ in order to sustain the vision of the radical lifestyle to which he calls us. But in the process of such disciplined effort, we actually become more self-aware, more loving, more thoughtful, and more insightful. In the long run, we bear what the apostle Paul calls the fruit of the Spirit: love, joy, peace, patience, kindness, generosity, faithfulness, gentleness, and self-control (Gal. 5:22–23).

Prayer

For some people, following Jesus is like holding an opinion: they sign on to his ideas, as they understand them, and try to mold their lives to his teaching. There are plenty of people who would not readily call themselves Christians, including most Muslims and even a few atheists, who agree that Jesus was a wise teacher and prophet and who try to internalize his spiritual and moral insights. It is important for Christians to remember that Jesus is not their property or the property of their religious tradition. He was a Jew, he is revered by Muslims, and he is precious to spiritually lively people in all cultures and religions. But it would not normally occur to such people to pray either to Jesus or to God in Jesus's name, as many Christians do. Such prayer is for people who want to follow Jesus Christ in a personal way that nurtures a relationship.

There are also many Christians who pray fervently to Jesus or to God in Jesus's name and sign on to very few of Jesus's ideas. It is as if their relationship with Jesus Christ has taken on a life of its own, and that relationship has more importance for them than what the Bible records about Jesus's teaching. That's how they wind up becoming exclusionary rather than radically inclusive, and how they manage to sanctify the economic and social practices of their own culture instead of applying Jesus's radical criteria for evaluating economic and social conditions. Making the Bible authoritative for Christian life means that Christians must constantly check their emotional and spiritual relationship with Jesus Christ against the biblically recorded memories of Jesus's earliest followers. We have learned enough about social and psychological dynamics thanks to the human sciences to understand how a relationship with Jesus Christ can flower in the right social setting with the right imaginative resources, yet with very little guidance from the Bible. Gut checks are important.

The moderate Christian instinctively grasps this tension between learning about Jesus from the Bible and a prayerful relationship with Jesus, whom they acknowledge as the Christ. They vary in personal style tremendously, of course, but their preference for moderation causes them to tend toward balance between the spiritual enthusiasm of prayer to or through Jesus, on the one hand, and the tentative knowledge of the person and work of Jesus as the Bible makes that available to us, on the other. The question for moderate Christians, then, is how to nurture a personal relationship with Jesus Christ through prayer without falling into the kind of excessive enthusiasm that fails utterly to come to terms with the challenge of Jesus's teaching.

The answer is to keep prayer and learning together, and to do so both corporately and individually. Learning and prayer both require practice and effort. Both condition one another, increasing love of the Bible and bringing challenging content to the relationship with Jesus Christ. Learning, in other words, is the partner of prayer. Together they constitute a conversation within which a meaningful relationship with Jesus Christ can grow.

For some moderate Christians, their relationship with Jesus Christ is intimate and personal and immediate. They picture prayer as a conversation with a living supernatural being that is present with them at every minute and able to communicate through events, thoughts, and even (at times) through words. It is particularly important for people who have such two-way experiences of prayer to stay aligned with the Bible so as to avoid the sort of misguided enthusiasm that Christian leaders have always roundly attacked as dangerous for faith. For example, when Jonathan Edwards strove to help the members of his congregation make sense of their intense experiences during the Great Awakening, he urged them to test those experiences and the enthusiastic convictions that resulted against common sense, traditional wisdom, and especially the Bible.

For other moderate Christians, prayer is a discipline of focused attention on God with elements of thanksgiving, confession, and intercession. It usually involves speaking or thinking or reading but sometimes includes wordless meditation. Prayer helps such Christians focus their attention on their responsibilities for the day. Such prayer would not normally be a two-way conversation in itself so these folk often combine prayer with Bible reading. And they usually talk to God, in the name of Jesus Christ, rather than directly to Jesus Christ. In other words, Jesus is their model for prayer, rather than the object of their prayer.

One of us once led a Christian discussion and prayer group with a focus on spirituality and vocation. On one memorable occasion, Linda spoke about her experience of prayer as literally a two-way conversation, in which she spoke and heard Jesus Christ's voice in her head. Phil piped up, wanting to know whether Linda was describing an extreme and rare experience, or whether this was common for her. Linda replied that this happened to her all the time, and added that she could not see what the point of prayer would be if it weren't a two-way conversation. The subsequent conversation revealed that nobody else in the group had experiences like those of Linda, but it also left some things unsaid that were clearly hovering in the room. Some were covertly jealous of Linda's experiences, being frustrated with the barren, one-sided quality of their own prayers. Others were worried about Linda's psychological stability. And almost everyone resented the way Linda depreciated their own less colorful experiences of prayer as pointless. It was a fascinating moment of shock and surprise as different perceptions, expectations, and backgrounds clashed.

Moderate Christian churches of the liberal-evangelical kind can expect to host this sort of diversity on the meaning and practice of prayer. It really is unnecessary for Christians to attack or depreciate others solely because of different experiences and understandings of prayer. The Christian movement has forever enjoyed such diversity and continues to do so today. Once people learn about these differences it is easier for them to find a way to conduct public prayer that is meaningful for everyone, and to profit from each other's spiritual insights, which are borne of surprisingly diverse spiritual practices. Part of learning to pray involves finding out about this diversity of spiritual practices, discussing the challenges and joys of prayer, and coming to understand the way different types of people gravitate to different styles of prayer.

What is more problematic than unnecessary conflict over prayer is not praying at all. This is surprisingly common in churches. If there is one thing that the Christian church should do differently than other organizations, it is stressing mindfulness of God. This should occur even (especially!) within its business meetings. Church meetings should begin and end in authentic and soul-searching prayer, to focus people's minds on the task at hand, and also to remind everyone that Christians try to live in such a way that their business can also be the business of the reign of God. Whenever Christians gather they should remind themselves of who, and whose, they are.

Service

Learning and prayer lead to action. The action may be undertaking lifestyle changes as a way of taking fuller responsibility for the world we share with six billion other people and a numberless host of other living beings. It may be changing charitable giving patterns. It may be forgiving an enemy or being more patient and loving at home. It may mean making banners and publicly protesting some form of social injustice. In all of these actions, Christians believe that they serve God's kingdom.

The aspiration to Christian service presents two challenges for discerning moderate Christians. On the one hand, it is difficult to know when to take a stand on the big issues of the day, and what stand to take, both as individuals and as groups. This is made more difficult by the painful fact that well-meaning Christians have been, and still are, on all sides of every hot-button issue, from abolition to abortion, from the economy to the environment, from wages to war. As we argued in part III, we think that congregations are the right context to sort out these debates, making use of resources from denominational and transdenominational organizations. These processes of discussion are opportunities for learning and also for the practice of discernment as a committed group of Christians struggling for a common vision.

This challenge makes it tempting to confine Christian service to the less controversial issues and to our private lives. But moderate Christians serious about radical discipleship must not fall prey to that temptation. The radical Christian disciple's mandate for action extends across the board, from the private to the public, and from noncontroversial lifestyle decisions to the flash points of cutting-edge social debate. Moreover, the Bible does take clear stands, especially on economic and social justice, and those ancient insights can be translated effectively into our economic circumstances and cultural context. So Christians must face, rather than avoid, the alarming fact that Christians disagree on almost everything. In doing so, it is not a compromise between the extremes but rather an imagination-transforming commitment to love that lifts the tone of debate and unearths the principles that lead to resolution.

On the other hand, some Christians are so engaged in the business of public Christian service that they forget the demands of radical discipleship for profound behavior change. This sort of personal quest for holiness is never completed, despite surprising claims to the contrary within the so-called holiness traditions such as Methodism and the Nazarene Church. It is also genuinely difficult for any human being to change his or her naturally selfish or thoughtless reactions to family and friends, colleagues and strangers. Some of that difficulty derives from the well-established psychological insight that personalities hardly ever change significantly. But within most personality types there are paths to holiness, to increased love and care, to decreased selfishness and anger. Buddhists have their Noble Eight-Fold Path, which reliably produces compassion and goodness. In the same way, Christians walk paths of radical discipleship and learn to bear the fruits of the Spirit in a daily discipline of focused attention through learning and prayer. Every positive action that results from this effort is an aspect of Christian service to God's kingdom.

Learning, prayer, and service are all essential disciplines for the Christian determined to follow Jesus Christ. Each requires its own skill set and we do not acquire any of those skills without focused effort. But the practice of these disciplines also brings a deep joy and a bracing freedom that is difficult to convey to the one who only sees the hard work and discipline required. Learning to see the world differently and to act in the world accordingly is no easy calling but it produces such wondrous fruits that the mature Christ-centered disciple cannot imagine longing to serve any other master.

CHAPTER 11

Radical Inclusiveness for Moderate Christians

WHAT'S RADICAL ABOUT CHRISTIAN INCLUSIVENESS?

Loving the Least of These

Jesus's parable of the sheep and the goats in the Gospel of Matthew (25:31–46) furnishes a basis for a Christian commitment to radical inclusiveness. In this story, Jesus pictures a universal judgment whose ruling criterion is how individuals take care of those who are considered the least—Jesus calls them "these brothers of mine," and we would add sisters as well. The least, the lowly, the poor, the marginalized, are Jesus's family; they are his people.

> I tell you the truth, whatever you did for one of the least of these brothers of mine, you did for me. (Matt. 25:40 NIV)

It is disturbing to comfortable, civilized, cultured Christians to hear that the people we tend to disregard are the very people Jesus regarded most highly. Yet that's the way the Gospels record it. His followers vividly recalled that Jesus regularly reached out to, spent time with, and even worked with those who the world views as insignificant. Sinners, tax collectors, poor beggars, the lame and blind, adulterers, fishermen, and even the filthy rich found their way to Jesus and he welcomed them with open arms and a challenging message of repentance and change. Jesus was radically inclusive. No one was outside his embrace, not even the wealthy or the politically powerful. The church of Jesus Christ should function in the same way. Everyone should be welcome into the presence of Jesus Christ, *especially* those whom society pushes out to the margins.

The radical inclusiveness of Jesus's ministry stands out in the call and sending forth of the disciples. Today, common business practice dictates that when a position is to be filled an employer should look for the best, brightest, most competent, and most dependable person for the job. Apparently Jesus never got the memo on that. The call of the disciples is remarkable for its simplicity and brevity. The Gospels record that Peter and Andrew, James and John, Matthew and Levi all heard Jesus say, "Follow me," after which they dropped what they were doing and followed. Taken at face value, these invitations don't make sense, and no doubt these young men had heard about Jesus before they saw him preaching and healing. Yet the gospel writers seem to relish recalling stories of how powerful Jesus's call was to those who heard it. "Come, follow me," doesn't seem a prudent or careful arrangement. Shouldn't Jesus at least have conducted a background check on these guys? Would it be asking too much to have asked each of them to submit a letter of application, or at least to present a few personal references? These invitations were going to lead to a seat at the Last Supper, so Jesus might have been a bit more discriminating. Even more striking are the Gospels' claims that Jesus knew these men were going to fail him.

All of that shows the beauty and power of Jesus's call. There are no background checks, and recommendations and references are not required. In fact, even a promise of future faithfulness does not appear to be necessary. The only thing that a person needs to be a disciple of Jesus Christ, according to the gospel story, is a willingness to follow. Jesus demonstrates a radical inclusiveness that bespeaks God's grace and love for our sinful and broken world.

Even if people are poor or poorly educated, even if they have failed in the past and are certain to fail in the future, even if they stand at the doorways of the world and are ignored, Jesus is ready to welcome them. This is grace held out for all people.

No one is beyond the bounds of Christ's love. Young, old, attractive, homely, able bodied, handicapped, rich, poor, gay, straight, PhD, GED, male, female, Jew, Gentile, sinner, saint, Republican, Democrat—according to the Gospels, everyone is welcome. This does not mean that Christians don't confront inappropriate or harmful behavior when necessary. Rather, the gospel message is to come *as you are,* so that Jesus Christ can transform you into what you *can be.*

Dealing with Institutional Realities

Sadly, radical inclusiveness is nearly impossible for human groups of any sort to implement. It is a particularly difficult challenge in groups of conservative Christians and in groups of liberal Christians, both of which heavily depend on ideological distinctiveness for their subcultural identity. Conservative Christians are clear that there are people who are outside the bounds of God's love. According to them, a whole lot of people are going to go to hell. If you are gay, if you are Muslim or Buddhist, if you haven't accepted Jesus Christ as your personal Lord and Savior, you are cut off from God's saving love. You will eventually be thrown into a sea of fire for all eternity. Conservative Christians may not think of it all that often, but theirs is a terrifyingly exclusive faith.

This brings to mind a woman who had grown up in a very conservative Christian church and now attends a liberal-evangelical church. She came to her pastor deeply concerned. She is married to a Jewish man, and while she has raised their three children in the Christian church, they still observe Shabbat and other Jewish traditions and holidays. She had just finished reading Rick Warren's book *The Purpose Driven Life,* and she was terrified that her husband and children where going to go to hell because they were Jewish. She cried, "I would rather be trying to protect my children in hell than be alone in heaven!"

Liberal Christians aren't much better. Most liberal Christians pride themselves on their inclusive nature and they bristle at the idea of an irrationally judgmental God who would cast anyone, let alone faithful Jews, into a sea of fire. However, theirs is not a truly inclusive faith either. At a very liberal church we know, gay and lesbian church members hold hands with straight men and women, and their children. Everyone is welcome, or so they say. Sermon after sermon is preached about God's love, and how all people are created in the image of God. It is a small community, and upon entering you feel as though you are part of the family. When the kids come up for the children's sermon, it looks as if it is a microcosm of how God's church should look. In this predominantly white neighborhood, the children of this church are a beautifully colored lot. There are kids from China, Nicaragua, Ecuador, Nigeria, and just about every other country from which gay and lesbian couples can successfully adopt children. At first glance, and even on the second and third glance, this church appears to be truly living out Jesus's radically inclusive call to relationship and discipleship . . . even though Jesus's name is rarely mentioned.

There is a catch, however. The sermons, prayers, and testimonies often ridicule the religious right and other religious conservatives. Jesse Helms, Pat Robertson, and Jerry Falwell are routinely the objects of impassioned verbal attacks in public and the butt of jokes in private. To a person, members of the church are viscerally angered by anyone who would exclude people from God's family. And yet, this church fosters it own kind of exclusionary practices. When push comes to shove, it is a church that has little or no room for people who believe differently than they do. Conservative Christians of any denomination, Christians with conservative politics in any political party, and even most evangelicals, have no place there. It is tolerant of everyone except the intolerant, and people that remind them of the intolerant, and that compromises their welcome.

Liberal-evangelical churches are defined by their attempt to implement the radical inclusiveness of Jesus's life and ministry in their communities. Because of their belief that everyone receives God's love, their evangelical desire for everyone to be reconciled with God, and their humility around matters of theological doctrine and political ideology, they deliberately craft inclusive communities that cut across the divisions that seem so inevitable and inviolable within the wider culture.

At a liberal-evangelical church we know, George, a conservative Republican, sits next to Janice, a Green Party peace advocate. Evangelical Christine holds hands with Unitarian Martha. Jason the UPS guy and Scott the investment banker converse with each other while watching their children run through the sanctuary after Sunday worship. Liberals, conservatives, evangelicals, Democrats, Republicans, the very young, and the very old all find a welcome in this church. The welcome is not one of mutual agreement on political or religious beliefs, because there is real disagreement there. It is rather that each person is respected as a child of God and as a disciple of Jesus Christ.

There are limits on Christian unity, as we described in *Lost in the Middle?* and again in part III above. Social groups can only take so much stress before they fly apart. We think that the liberal-evangelical church cannot survive if biblical literalism takes center stage to accommodate conservative evangelicals. Nor can it afford to sacrifice Christ-centeredness to keep secular liberals happy. Moreover, local social and economic contexts largely determine the kinds of inclusiveness for which churches can strive. While the church strives to be inclusive in every way, in some contexts the most immediate challenge will be inclusiveness across race, in others socioeconomic status, in yet others sexual orientation or age or ethnic subculture or language. Without focusing on one kind of inclusiveness to the exclusion of others, a liberal-evangelical church should pay close attention to its actual local setting and craft a testimony to divine love through radical inclusiveness in the ways their setting most needs.

In almost all places, moderate Christians committed to radical inclusiveness can target divisions deriving from conflicting political ideologies and theological worldviews. It is in these areas of political and religious conviction, particularly, that the liberal-evangelical church can take a stand against polarization in public discourse and help people to understand differently minded others. In this and every other way that the church models Jesus's radical inclusiveness, it testifies to the power of divine love to unite human beings across the inevitable divisions of society and politics.

How Do Moderate Christians
Nurture Radical Inclusiveness?

We have suggested that realizing the ideal of radical inclusiveness within church institutions is difficult. There are conflicts
small and large to manage, personalities that seem to drag down
every idealistic vision, problems with budgets and programs to
solve, and a never-ending litany of irritations to frustrate the best
efforts of church leaders. Any church leader who visits a decent
Christian bookstore will scan the shelves and quickly discover
how they might research techniques for purpose-driven churches, growing churches, and financially successful churches. How
do moderate Christians nurture the countercultural ideal of radical inclusiveness within their local churches? We discuss three
key elements of the answer to this question in what follows.

Worship and Sacraments

What happens when Christians gather together is the single most
important factor in defining Christian identity. That fact marks
the importance of worship for everything that Christians do and
are, including whether they will value the ideal of radical inclusiveness.

Some people who put worship services together do so almost
robotically, using standard forms without much reflection or understanding, and plugging holes in an order of worship to get
one more task out of their inbox. There is some wisdom in trusting established forms of Christian worship because they have
been honed through constant usage and evaluation over centuries. But the robotic, hole-plugging approach to the task badly
misjudges the importance of Christian worship. Every single
worship service presents opportunities to educate and inspire, to
bring comfort and healing, to unite families across generations,
to set forth a vision of Christian duty and service, to raise consciousness about injustice and the transformative power of love,
to challenge the religion of cultural convenience, and to define
congregational identity. With so much at stake, worship design-
ers and leaders have enormous responsibility.

As far as radical inclusiveness is concerned, the question is whether Christian worship manifests it. Do the prayers surprise people with concern for the Other that they rarely consider? Do the hymns and songs reinforce tribal stereotypes or open people's eyes to the diversity of creation and human cultures? Do the greetings make the congregation aware of their precious diversity and the immovable generosity of Christ's welcome?

One of the reasons that Mahatma Gandhi was so skeptical about Christianity, despite his love for Jesus and his respect for Jesus's teaching, is an experience he had as a young lawyer in South Africa. Curious about Christianity, he tried to enter a church service to find out more. A white church elder prevented him from entering. The dark-skinned Gandhi explained that he wanted to attend worship. The elder replied, "There's no room for kaffirs in this church." Gandhi was not the first non-Christian to appreciate the inclusive welcome of Jesus Christ and yet want nothing to do with the church's exclusionary way of being Christians at worship. There are many people alive today who feel much the same way, including a fair portion of the so-called Revolutionary Christians we discussed in part III.

The sacraments are among the most important moments in Christian worship, so the way they are conducted says a lot about whether a congregation grasps the meaning of radical inclusiveness. This is especially true of baptism and Holy Communion, which are both explicitly welcoming, community events. Baptism is a welcome into Christ's family and Holy Communion a welcome to Christ's table of fellowship. To celebrate together the reception of a person into Christ's family through baptism is a profound point of contact for ideologically, morally, theologically, and culturally diverse Christians. Likewise, to approach the Table of the Lord in order to share a symbolic meal together prompts Christians to set aside their ordinary concerns and habits of mind and to regard their Christian family with acceptance and thanksgiving.

The sacramental life of the church opens us to the presence of Christ. Through baptism and communion we encounter the memory and spirit of Christ in uniquely powerful ways. More and more Protestant churches are celebrating Holy Communion with increasing regularity. Pastors often comment that the sacrament of Holy Communion helps to balance a worship service. In fact, pastors acknowledge that communion helps to alleviate the pressure of the sermon moment itself. When the sacraments are allowed to be the sacraments, and the sermon sheds its pseudo-sacramental role in Protestant worship, the focus shifts from the preacher to the body, blood, and spirit of Christ. This realignment is true to the calling of Christ, and clergy and laity alike can sense the "rightness" of it all.

When framed thoughtfully, Christian sacraments are powerful relativizing forces. They reduce pride of identity and arrogance of opinion and replace them with simple concern and care. They show people that most of the things they feel strongly about are actually secondary. Love matters more. Christians learn about radical inclusiveness best by enacting it in worship and sacraments.

Preaching and Visionary Leadership

Pastoral leadership that is committed to a radically inclusive welcome is essential to maintain what might otherwise be tenuous relationships among diverse Christians. Without such visionary leadership, moments of worship and the sacraments themselves may never manifest Christ's boundless welcome. The pastor of the liberal-evangelical church realizes that doubting Thomas, denying Peter, betraying Judas, and all the deserting disciples were still welcome in Jesus's presence. No one, not even Judas, was refused a place at the Lord's Table. Liberal-evangelical pastors are always most concerned to help people to find their place at the table, after which they trust that God will meet them where they are and take them where they need to go. Liberal-evangelical church leaders steer away from judgmental self-righteousness by focusing on the *log in their own eyes* while leaving judgment to God.

Above all, it is in the moment of Christian public speaking that preachers give words to the meaning of Christian welcome in their congregations. If worship and sacraments set the tone for radical inclusiveness, then sermons declare the theme. Discipleship and membership in God's human family is the common ground on which this kind of welcome is extended and sermons have to spell out that vision. This is no small challenge. A radically inclusive welcome is a subversive act that runs against the tide of all of the tribal forces of human groups. No matter how inclusive a church tries to be, however, the human condition is such that there will always be limits on group identity. We have discussed some of those limits in the case of the liberal-evangelical community—including not compromising the centrality of Christ and the rejection of biblical literalism. We believe that those limits need to be explained in thoughtful sermons, right along with the reason why those limits should not interfere with an expansive Christ-like welcome of all people into the family of God, and onto the path of Christian discipleship.

Such sermons stretch people uncomfortably. In some conservative churches they just don't fly because most people there prize doctrinal purity above inclusive love, or seek the artificial clarity of biblical literalism rather than the complex authority of a life-long relationship with the Bible. In some liberal churches, sermons about radical inclusiveness are welcome only up to the point that the preacher spells out what it means: that all people belong, even those with what some might consider bad politics or others might judge as inappropriately enthusiastic spirituality. It is the very definition of the liberal-evangelical setting that most Christians there prize being stretched in this way. They seek out and count on hearing such a message. So it is especially in those settings that preachers can and must make clear the reasoning behind a Christ-like radically inclusive welcome and its importance for contesting the tribalism of a religiously and ideologically polarized culture.

Local Congregational Narratives

Over time, habits of radical inclusiveness within a community of Christians spontaneously forge a local congregational narrative. People understand their church and their Christian commitment in terms of radically inclusive love and talk to each other naturally about it. They recognize the marks of that commitment in the worship service and in the way they conduct the sacraments.

They start to internalize the reasoning for this approach to life that they have heard in sermons. They seek out leadership that will support their vision of Christian community. They naturally come to think of their local congregation as a beacon of light that testifies to the power of love—power to transform self-protective instincts and to unite people across the seemingly unbridgeable chasms of culture, politics, and theological worldview.

Sociologist Nancy Ammerman has shown in her *Pillars of Faith* that local corporate narratives are a vital component in the framing of congregational identity. These narratives help to maintain identity in the midst of culturally reinforced tendencies toward fragmentation and confusion. They support the self-understandings, social bonds, spiritual traditions, and wider community connections that sustain religious faith in a pluralistic society. It is in part because sociologists underestimated the power of local congregational narratives that the prominent sociological models of the twentieth century failed to predict the liveliness of contemporary Christianity, and instead predicted the triumph of secularism over all forms of religiousness. Reliance on secularization theories and rational choice principles meant that these sociologists simply could not explain communities that flourish by narrating stories and nurturing practices that say who they are and what they stand for. Criteria for plausibility do not fall from heaven. They are carried along within traditions, perpetuating themselves and adapting to social changes on the backs of local narratives and practices that define and relate a wider religious tradition to the concerns of living religious people. The older secularization-theory sociologists got it wrong because they misjudged how persuasive living narratives are to people for whom those narratives define a world of meaning and a life calling.

Liberal-evangelical local congregational narratives are diverse but they have one element in common. Their Christ-centeredness leads directly to a radical inclusiveness that runs against the grain of social divisions, hierarchies, and authority structures. Everyone in the congregation learns this, treasures it, and strives to act on it. And this is the way a radically inclusive congregational identity is forged in the midst of ideological and theological pluralism.

CHAPTER 12

Radical Ethics for Moderate Christians

WHAT'S RADICAL ABOUT CHRISTIAN ETHICS?

Comparative religions expert Huston Smith once described Christianity as a "brilliantly lit *bhakti* highway toward God." He was thinking of the diverse spiritual paths of Hinduism, of which just one is the path of devotion to God, or *bhakti*. This is a keen observation. Christianity is dominated by the ideal of love: God's love for the world, Jesus's love for his disciples, his disciples love for one another, and Christian love for the suffering and the poor. This is not merely the love of friendship but *agape* love, or unconquerable benevolence that unselfishly seeks the well-being of others, even strangers, and even enemies.

In the Chinese setting, the Neoconfucian revival had a great deal to do with transcending limited loyalties to family, tribe, and nation and seeking to complement these with a universal regard for human beings and all of nature. In Judaism the Abrahamic covenant was explicitly for the sake of all nations, not just for the tribes of Israel. Islamist extremism in the contemporary world masks Islam's traditional stress on everyone's equality before God. It is on the basis of this conviction, and some fortuitous political circumstances, that the Islamic civilization of Andalusian Spain managed for a couple of centuries to host virtually the only peaceful multireligious and multiethnic society in medieval Europe. The outward-looking, other-regarding, antitribalistic ideal of *agape* love is something that people in every culture and at every place and time have been able to conjure, even if

they have concluded that it is an unrealistic goal except in special circumstances. But Christians centralize this ideal at the core
of their ethical outlook and see it as embodied both in the life
and ministry of Jesus and in God's work of reconciling the world
through Christ.

Sadly, the Christian church and Christians alike have always
struggled to live up to the *agape* ideal, falling prey to the temptation to limit the scope of caring to family or community, to race
or culture. These forms of love may be wonderful on the inside
of the group but they routinely lead to cruel exclusion or devastating tribalistic violence toward outsiders. Christians too often
deserve the condemnation that Gandhi once so gently gave to
his friend, the famous evangelist E. Stanley Jones, when Jones
asked Gandhi why he was not a Christian despite his affection
for Jesus. Gandhi replied, "I like your Christ; I do not like your
Christians. Your Christians are so unlike your Christ." In fact,
Gandhi appreciated many works of love among Christians, so
this famous quote is slightly misleading as to his actual opinion
of the followers of Christ. But it certainly does issue a sharp challenge to Christians to live up to the ideals of the one they follow,
and to be far more radical in their discipleship.

Why is there such a yawning gap between the ideal of *agape*
love and the on-the-ground reality of Christian group life? Aside
from all of the sociological reasons for human self-protectiveness
that we have mentioned in previous chapters, there are extremely
sharp and eminently reasonable questions about the feasibility of
agape love as a social, political, economic, and military strategy.
Can an *agape* approach really work in hardscrabble elections to
political office, or as a social policy to replace the more common
policy of rewarding competence and punishing laziness? Can an
agape approach really protect Americans, the American economy, and the American way of life? Even most Christians seem
to agree that Christ's commandment to love in the *agape* sense
does not apply to our economic rivals and our military enemies.
Are we really supposed to turn the other cheek in *agape*-like self-
sacrifice in such cases? Wars are about survival and freedom, just
as the free-market economy is about competition and initiative,
and there is no place for *agape* in either case.

To grasp the alleged impracticality of *agape* in more detail, consider a Christian military strategist working as an adviser in the Pentagon; in fact, there are quite a few such folk. Can this person, having absorbed the previous Sunday's sermon on *agape* love and the Christian ethic of peace, safely raise *agape* as a consideration in a military strategy meeting? Can this adviser suggest that massive aid for children in Africa would be a better response to an enemy's violent attack than going to war? The answer, sadly, is almost certainly not. To begin with, there is little or no research literature against which claims about an *agape* military strategy could be assessed. There is a large body of literature on Gandhi's and King's active nonviolence but little of that exists in the context of military strategy. More than this, however, this Christian military strategist would expect to be called naive and foolish for proposing such an *agape* strategy. Someone would explain that the *agape* policy would make the United States look weak and afraid, after which it would be a laughingstock, soon destroyed by the violent tides of history that spare no quarter for kindness and understand only force. The fool that seriously proposes such a policy, be it a Pentagon official or Jesus Christ himself, has no business making decisions of vital national interest. That's what would be said. The military is all about force and is essentially violent; there is no room for *agape* love by definition.

This is the sense in which Western culture is only partly Christianized, and indeed why all cultures can never be brought into complete harmony with an *agape* approach to life. *Agape* love is essentially and inevitably and permanently countercultural. Nothing shows that more clearly than the fact of Jesus's death, and the unjust, illegal, and cruel character of his trial and execution. *Agape* asks people to love others more than themselves while human civilization is all about protecting resources for flourishing cultures.

An *agape* military policy or an *agape* approach to political elections may be foolish, in one way. But the radical Christian disciple is primed by the Bible, tradition, and experience to see wisdom within such foolish ideals—wisdom that others, whether Christian or not, tend to miss. For example, an *agape* military policy based on foreign aid instead of war, when consistently elaborated in other foreign and domestic policies, might have extraordinary effects. The United States's stature as a leader in world affairs would be strengthened formidably. Its form of government would suddenly be attractive to other countries rather than increasingly repulsive, which is often the effect of a militarily oriented foreign policy. It could save money while allowing the money involved to be spent in a much more constructive way. It would not be an easy path because it would involve a lot of explaining and education, and military hawks would resist it. But *agape* is never easy.

Despite the difficulties, and the lack of research into the viability of *agape* principles in social, political, economic, and military policies, discerning Christians should ponder it anyway. They should do this not because it is practical but because it begins to disclose precisely how radical is the *agape* approach to life. It shows how there can be wisdom hidden within what the world views as foolishness. It shows that Christianity too often simply abandons its own core ethical ideals and lines up behind the values of the wider culture. Once that happens, religious enthusiasm joins with nationalistic fervor and the cause of Christ is pushed aside, as he himself was temporarily pushed aside by the storming hooves of history. Even when there is no discernible practical value in practicing *agape* love, even when talking the talk has become impossible, the Christian's calling is to walk the walk anyway.

How Do Moderate Christians Live Out Radical Ethics?

The ethics of *agape* love seems diametrically opposed to the basic principles of civilization and to cultural survival and flourishing. Often enough, even the most discerning Christians can't see the wisdom hidden within what seems foolish to the worldly wise. So what practically can they do to live out the radical ethics of *agape*? What does radical discipleship mean here? We will consider just three issues, very briefly. In each case, we will argue that there is some wisdom that Christians can learn to see in the *agape* strategies that others mock as naive, and that Christians can take a principled stand even when they do not fully grasp the practical consequences of their actions.

Prosperity and Justice

Evangelicals in the United States used to be Democrats, on the whole. This was decades ago, back in the days when evangelical religious interests lined up with the religious commitment of the Democratic Party to the biblical values of caring for the poor and homeless, widows and orphans. Times have changed. Evangelical Christians, except for African Americans, are now more often Republicans. That's because evangelical religious interests align more with the Republican Party's stress on conserving moral and institutional values than with anything the Democratic Party is saying.

Meanwhile, as the evangelical center migrated from the middle left to the middle right on the political spectrum, two political transformations occurred with devastating results. On the one hand, Democrats made a play for the middle class of America and forsook their commitment to the poor, thereby surrendering the last vestige of plainspoken, everyone-gets-it, just-like-Jesus biblical values. On the other hand, Republicans embraced the self-reliance paradigm, with its welfare-makes-them-lazy corollary and the trickle-down economic theory that takes care of everyone by making sure that the wealthy are in good shape first. The devastating result? Neither of the two major U.S. political parties speaks for the poor any longer and evangelicals are in a moral crisis on this issue. Liberal Christians are still speaking for the poor, but they have been outflanked politically and religiously and have lost the impact that made them a force to be reckoned with in the post–World War II era of U.S. politics.

When we say devastating, that's exactly what we mean. Among wealthy democratic nations, the United States has the highest poverty rate, the largest prison population, and the highest rate of imprisonment. It has shockingly high rates of violent crime, drug addiction, infant mortality, families without health insurance, and gun deaths. It has intractable problems with health care delivery and social services. All of these problems, without exception, are tied to poverty.

Jim Wallis and a few other socially active evangelicals are keeping alive the flame of social activism that burned much more brightly in earlier generations. But no matter how much they and their liberal Christian counterparts thump the sermonic tub about the Bible's portrayal of Jesus's and indeed God's preference for the poor, the message does not get through. Now and then there are hopeful signs. For example, Rick Warren of Saddleback Church has begun championing the position that Christians need to serve the poor. The group known as Evangelicals for Social Action is inspiring progressive evangelicals to commit to social justice and environmental action. In general, however, Christianity in the United States has failed terribly on this issue. Well-known evangelical Ron Sider has published a book whose title says it all: *The Scandal of Evangelical Politics: Why Are Christians Missing the Chance to Really Change the World?* Never has a message so clear and so biblically dominant been so utterly ignored by Christians with the power to influence political policy.

Radical discipleship in this case is not terribly complicated. Governments of the last two decades might not like it but they are so far on the wrong side of the biblical criterion for social and economic justice that they are not even appearing in the sheep-and-goats judgment story of Matthew 25:31–46, which we discussed earlier in this chapter. They are off to the side somewhere, amusing themselves with their quarterly investment statements and debating fine points of morality, and not even trying to explain themselves to the indignant Judge. Notice what is and is not a criterion for judgment in this story. Positions on hot-button issues are not a basis for judgment. Denominational resolutions, a person's voting history, and having the right mission statement do not matter. There are no questions about what positions people hold regarding abortion, gay marriage, or the Israel-Palestine conflict. According to this parable, the Judge doesn't care about what a person *believes*, but what a person actually *does*. And judgment is rendered on a person's care of the least.

Now there are other biblical perspectives on salvation but we ignore this one at our peril. The biblical message about caring for the poor is so clearly the dominant ethical message of both the Hebrew Bible and the New Testament, and so densely present in the pages of the whole Bible, that the Christian's obligation is absolutely obvious.

So much for obligations. But is there a strategic aspect to the biblical picture that could help convince politicians and policy wonks that one-sided emphasis on the self-reliance paradigm is actually counterproductive? Is there, in other words, wisdom hidden in the idea of a strong government safety net, which currently seems both unfashionable to the trendy and foolish to the worldly wise? Indeed there is, and it is past time that Christians communicated clearly about this to their political leaders.

Jeffrey Sachs, Director of the Earth Institute at New York's Columbia University, has argued that the core working conviction of fiscal conservatives—what we are defining as the conjunction of trickle-down economics and a self-reliance ideology that sees welfare as nurturing weakness—is mistaken. Fiscal conservatives *assume* that the higher taxation needed to support a strong social safety net (e.g., unemployment protection, child support, health care funding, education spending) is incompatible with a free-market economy and produces a culture of laziness and dependence. But evidence from other democratic nations with free-market economies exists. And that evidence shows that this assumption is *false*. In fact, a strong social-welfare state reduces the terrible moral and financial costs associated with poverty and a huge prison population, while supporting fairness and competitiveness in international trade.

In other words, Christians can argue for political support for the biblical principle to care first for the poor not just on the basis of sentiment and religious conviction but also on the basis of comparative economic and social analysis. But whether the United States deals with its obligations to the poor through a thousand non-profit points of light, through a far more robust social-welfare system, or by doing nothing at all, the radical Christian disciple's obligation to the poor and downtrodden, to the prisoner and the ill, to widows and orphans, remains the same.

War and Peace

In discussing an *agape* approach to international conflict, above, we speculated about the wisdom of an *agape* policy diametrically opposed to the worldly wisdom that dominates military strategy and international relations. The same kinds of considerations apply to larger questions of war and peace. The wisdom of the *agape* policy is easiest to see in cases where the enemy is a populist movement that depends on resentment to fuel recruitment, as in the case of Islamist extremists, or when the enemy is a massively outnumbered foreign military power strongly constrained, most of the time, by an ethics of decency, as in the case of Gandhi's confrontation with the colonial British power in India. The nonviolent, turn-the-other-cheek approach of the *agape* policy can take the wind out of the sails of opponents in such situations.

But what about situations in which massive military might is wielded by a government with invasion, regime change, and comprehensive cultural imposition and transformation in mind? This was the case with the Third Reich in World War II. Gandhi recognized the difference between that situation and his own Indian independence movement, but still believed that there had to be a way that active nonviolence could win the day. We are not so sure. We suspect that a nonviolent *agape* policy in World War II from the Allies would have resulted in a German Europe. Of course, people would have lived on, learning the new national German language. But Jews and Gypsies and homosexuals and the mentally or physically disabled would have been murdered in the name of a scientifically bogus vision of racial purity. Cultural resources of inestimable value would have been lost—cultures that are preserved today because the Allies defended themselves and fought back with great violence and imagination, sacrifice and skill.

Perhaps the conclusion we should draw here is that the *agape* principle is too alien to the natural interests of civilizations and cultures to be of any use in formulating attitudes to issues of war and peace. We think that would be a legitimate conclusion, just as we can imagine authentically resisting this conclusion. But none of that changes the fact that Christians are commanded to love as Jesus loved, to take up their crosses and to follow him. Thus, even if there is no practical *agape* policy in situations of great social evil, radical Christian disciples still must decide about their personal role in war and as peacemakers. Many have chosen pacifism, and many others medical work, in response to their convictions about war and peace in light of Jesus's example. Some chose to fight and kill, often at the cost of terrible injuries or death, believing that to fight would bring long-lasting peace. In all cases, however, the radical Christian disciple must confront questions of war and peace with Christ's command clearly in mind. The Christian firing a gun at a distant enemy may seem the same as anyone else doing the same thing, but the motivations should be significantly different. Likewise, the Christian pacifist may seem similar to a cynical draft-dodging pacifist, but the motivations will be poles apart, as will their respective abilities to make peace.

Ecology and the Future

As a final example of how to live out the radical Christian ethics of *agape* in a complicated world, consider the many individual ecological catastrophes of human making. It is a depressing list, really, from accelerating extinctions to global warming. The science on all of this has been beyond question for many years. Scientists constantly debate the details but not the central claims. It is now virtually impossible to find a reputable scientist who is willing to deny that human beings are contributing significantly to global warming in a way that is potentially disastrous for human interests. An individual government may not want to accept the economic consequences of this dawning realization, and indeed some governments (such as the USA) have refused to accept reports from their own scientific advisory boards in an effort to avoid responsibility, but that will pass quickly because the scientific consensus is so overwhelming. Human civilization is heading down a dangerous path with no clear idea about how to change direction, and sooner or later everyone will see this clearly.

What this means for the radical Christian disciple is quite complicated. For Christians who set their eyes on a world of greater reality, beauty, and importance than this one, a world into which they will be welcomed upon their deaths, it is really quite difficult to get terribly worried about ecological disasters. It is a vale of tears and passing shadows, after all. Even Jesus speaks this way sometimes, though not in relation to ecological problems so much as in regard to the suffering of ordinary life and his disciples's longing to be with their master. The apostle Paul seems thoroughly confident in most of his writings that the world is about to end. He advised Christians not to get married (unless they couldn't control their sexual desires) and not to worry about earthly possessions, but rather to fix their eyes on the prize and endure whatever sufferings they must on the way to glory.

Moderate Christians get worried about this sort of apocalyptic, otherworldly enthusiasm, and not just because Paul was obviously wrong about his expectations for his immediate future. They also recall the creation story in which God declares the creation good and blesses it (Genesis 1). They trust their experiences of nature's beauty and majesty, and appreciate even its terrifying and dangerous aspects. If such moderates look for a better world of conscious experience after death, they still find themselves unable to ignore the biblical charge to be good stewards of this world.

Practically speaking, that settles the decision for the Christian disciple. Regardless of how much Christians long for a better world, we are commanded to be stewards of this one. Stewardship is not merely focused on human interests; it means conserving environments, protecting endangered species and genetic diversity, restricting anthropogenic influences to reasonable levels, and reducing pollution.

In light of the radical Christian *agape* ethic, however, stewardship can take on another level of meaning. The other-regard of *agape* naturally extends from human beings to other animals and to plants and even ecosystems and landscapes. Saint Francis of Assisi is the famous model in this regard. His love for animals and all of nature was a direct consequence of his love for God.

It follows that Christian disciples need not confine themselves to making environmental policy decisions based only on human interests. *Agape* is as wide as all of nature, because it is the love of the living creator God.

A MODERATE CONCLUSION

If you are a moderate Christian of the liberal and evangelical type, you are probably deeply attracted to the prospect of breathing life into radical Christian spiritual and ethical principles in your context. But you may also be harboring a niggling worry about language, namely, that being simultaneously moderate and radical sounds self-contradictory. It is that word "moderate"; it just doesn't sound very exciting. That is a sign of the times: we seem to believe that the only people who can be radical are ideologically and theologically extreme. But that is just not so, and here's why in a nutshell.

We have argued that the religious extremes of our context actually adopt variations of compromised culture Christianity. In other words, they sell out the radically inclusive and systemically challenging implications of Jesus's ministry and message for the sake of economic comfort and cultural convenience. These are worthy goals from some points of view; after all, we all want safety and security, good health care and fulfilling activities, clean water and readily available food. If belonging to a church can help with that, then so much the better. And if we have to break into like-minded groups and neglect prophetic analyses of unjust economies and arrogant international relations, then that is a price most of us are more than willing to pay. Culture Christianity is a religion of convenience that confirms our cultural habits and blunts the force of Jesus's radically inclusive, culturally topsy-turvy message.

In such a context, moderate Christians who resist the extremes and commit themselves to Christ-centered inclusiveness and the *agape* principle *are the radicals*. They go back to the roots (that's what "radical" means) of the Christian movement, drawing inspiration from Jesus and from the men and women who were his first followers. So grounded and guided, they see the contemporary world differently. They see beyond culture wars and religious animosity to the depths of the human condition, from which conflict springs all too quickly and violently. Jesus engaged the exquisite agonies of human life with open arms and transformative love, and discerning disciples of Jesus Christ have labored to do the same in every time since and in every place that the Christian gospel has reached.

In fact, at the extremes of religious polarization, it is easier to be fashionable and controversial than to be truly radical. It is discerning moderate Christians who can best sense and respond to the radical calling of the Christian way. Their location in the middle might make them feel lost at times but it is a blessing in disguise. With the right support, they learn to feel at home in the middle, and they feel grateful for the wise instincts that lead them to resist the extremes of left and right and to go deep instead.

PART V

Guide for the Perplexed

CHAPTER 13

A Guide for Discerning Moderate Christians

Techniques of congregational management and renewal are blind without theological insight, even as theology is lame without practical strategic thinking. So we present here a compact, seven-point guide for moderate Christians with liberal and evangelical instincts, and for the liberal-evangelical churches they seek to nurture. Each theme pairs a core conviction with a strategic response. Each of the seven themes summarizes a key practical implication of this book, especially in relation to looking to the future for guidance about how moderate Christians can live lives of countercultural discipleship in Christ-centered, radically inclusive, *agape*-oriented churches.

EVANGELICAL REPENTANCE

The modern history of the word "evangelicalism" began with an act of semantic theft, turning the evangel, the gospel, into a club with which to beat one's opponents. That sort of thing is fun when you are winning and it makes for intense togetherness when under fire. But it is still theft, massively narrowing the sense of the gospel, and suppressing legitimate diversity in the name of rationalizing local group identity. Like our fathers told us, after we take things that are not ours, we have to give them back.

Core Conviction:
We need to repent of our attempts to control the gospel.

We all long to be comfortable but the gospel discomfits as much as it comforts. This should be no surprise for Protestants because of their commitment to perpetual reformation.

Strategic Response:
Admit pluralism in the core message and
practices of Christianity.

The truly ugly history of Protestant church splits sends a clear message: basing church identity on doctrine when the Bible is your authoritative source will always lead to splits because the Bible does not say one thing. We earn moral and spiritual orientation through a discerning conversation among plural voices, including biblical, traditional, and contemporary wisdom.

LIBERAL REPENTANCE

The modern history of the word "liberal" carries forward its medieval associations with class and privilege, whereby only the free could learn what they wanted and form their own opinions openly and honestly. In our time, this has become a cultural form of condescension. Supposedly only high-culture, high-brow, high-minded liberals can face the truth about group-identity-destroying core-message pluralism. Everyone else needs the group identity more than they love the truth. Like our mothers told us, after we are rude to someone, we have to say sorry.

Core Conviction:
We need to repent of the condescension that links class to
religious courage, and culture to religious honesty.

Learning confers great advantages of understanding and sweetly complicates every part of our lives. But learning does not go with class and culture. It goes with opportunity and discipline.

Strategic Response:
Prioritize education.

Liberal-evangelical churches must stress education generally and Christian education specifically. They must work to create opportunities for learning and to cultivate the spiritual and emotional disciplines needed to make the most of those opportunities.

WORSHIP IS THE BOND

When we allow the pluralism of the Christian movement to register in the core message of a church, we definitely weaken the glue that keeps everyone together. Liberal-evangelicals have to find a way to strengthen the glue of social unity even while admitting core-message pluralism.

Core Conviction:
We need to recognize that worship and sacraments hold the church together better than doctrines and beliefs.

As humbling as this may be for Protestants, we need to learn this lesson from the great Catholic mother church. Liberal-evangelical churches must centralize worship and sacraments, and place doctrine in a subordinate, though still essential, position. And not just any worship will do.

Strategic Response:
Strive for excellence in public worship.

Energetic worship and inspiring sacraments can artfully encompass every dimension of human beings. Gifted leaders of worship know how to ease people out of their comfort zones and into new reaches of their own spiritual potential. They know how to steady those whose enthusiasm outruns their discipline. They understand how the sacraments bind Christians together despite their differences of opinions in politics and theology.

MESSAGE MATTERS

When the pastor steps into the pulpit to preach the gospel, the rubber meets the road. Will we hear vague nonsense or spiritual paralysis in the face of a profound intellectual challenge? Will we hear a muddled message presented as if we are supposed to find it exciting, or shallow moral maxims that mask all-important details? If so, liberal-evangelical Christianity in the twenty-first century is just a foolish dream.

Core Conviction:
We need to proclaim that God was present in Jesus Christ,
reconciling the world.

This is a truly excellent story. We can meditate on Jesus's life and teaching, and notice the life-changing effects he had on his followers, as well as on his enemies. We can trace out the way his followers struggled to understand how Jesus's power to change lives continued after his death, how God could work through him apart from his physical presence. We can ponder the marvelous theories of reconciliation that shift with every worldview and culture that Christianity passed through. We can wonder at the way Christianity always existed in translation, always adapted to new contexts, and always drew forth new ideas as the core message of the gospel passed across cultures and eras. Through it all, with no need to oversimplify, and no shortage of excitement, God has been in Jesus Christ, reconciling the world. This message preaches, it opens up onto a world full of religions, and it invites Christians to educate themselves about that world and their own wondrously diverse faith heritage.

Strategic Response:
Strive for excellence in preaching.

Having a message that preaches doesn't help unless preachers of the word know their Bible and theology, work hard in preparation, bring spiritual vibrancy into the pulpit, and love their people. None of that happens by accident. It requires a lot of learning and precise feedback, along with a great deal of effort and practice.

Vibrant Spirituality

What about spirituality for liberal-evangelicals? Where is the internal fire that sparks fellowship, heals the ravages of sin, breaks addictions, inspires forgiveness, and makes us strong to love God, others, and ourselves? Liberal-evangelical Christianity is not just a gospel *about* Jesus Christ; it is a relationship *with* Jesus Christ.

Core Conviction:
We need to keep our eyes fixed on Jesus Christ.

Following Jesus Christ each day of our lives is more important than being able to explain on demand the doctrine of the Trinity or the Hypostatic Union. Remembering Jesus in the Holy Eucharist is more important than being able to define the real presence or whatever it is that keeps Christians coming back ever and again to the communion table. Trusting that God was in Jesus Christ reconciling the world, making us at-one with God, is more important than being able to justify our favorite theory of the at-one-ment (the literal meaning of "atonement"). When the Christian keeps his or her eyes fixed on Jesus, the back gets straighter, the spirit gets stronger, the joy gets deeper, and the task of faithful Christian living gets clearer.

Strategic Response:
Seek a personal relationship with Jesus Christ through prayer, biblically guided meditation, and spiritual disciplines.

All relationships need work as well as inspiration. Liberal-evangelical Christians must pray, and so they must learn the art of prayer. They must meditate on the stories of Jesus's life and so they must learn to read and become comfortable within the strange new world of the Bible. They must find a spiritual path on which to follow Jesus and so they must learn about the Christian church's vast variety of spiritual disciplines, each tuned to different personality types and contexts.

KINGDOM MISSION

What does spirituality mean when we leave church? What do we do at work, at home, in the voting booth, in social action? How do we avoid the current evangelical trap of neglecting Jesus's command to prioritize the poor and marginalized, and the current liberal trap of understanding our own salvation in terms of the good works we do?

Core Conviction:
God's mission of *agape* love and justice is our mission.

Discerning Christians are invited into God's mission of reconciliation by extending God's love in Christ to others. We can't love others in the name of Jesus Christ unless we struggle with them to achieve justice, health, and healing. Social justice and evangelism are essential components of the Christian church's mission within the far wider and in fact boundless mission of God's kingdom.

Strategic Response:
Explicitly link social activism with spiritual life.

Social action is a spiritual practice because it is part of God's mission in Christ that has taken root within the life of the Christian church. The social work of discerning Christians is not merely a way to keep busy; it is an outworking of our love and gratitude to God whose mission has transformed our lives, and our response to love others as we would ourselves most long to be loved.

REVERENT HUMILITY

God's being far surpasses our cognitive and spiritual ability to comprehend. Beyond our church there are other churches, beyond Christianity there are other spiritual communities, beyond our understandings there are other deep visions of the truth.

Core Conviction:
We must humbly and thankfully confess that God's Spirit
moves in every place, every time, and every way.

God is not tamed by our insecurities or confined by our imaginations. God's truth is not exhausted by our doctrines and access to God is not controlled by our sacramental gateways. Our God images are always too small and the reach of God's grace broader and deeper than we can conceive. Ignorance of the Other for the sake of comfort and clear identity is nothing more than neglect of another part of God's creation.

Strategic Response:
Make humility a blessed thing by embodying it in
ecumenical openness and radical inclusiveness.

Liberal-evangelical Christians and churches define themselves by a God that can't be tamed and a divine mission that exceeds our grasp and understanding, despite our grateful participation in it. This blessed humility inspires the radical inclusiveness of the Christian gospel, breaking boundaries of class and culture and reaching out in transforming love across political and religious differences. The humble power of radically inclusive *agape* heals and transforms more surely than arrogant force.

CHAPTER 14

Parting Words: What's Next?

In closing, we offer thoughts specifically for three subgroups within our intended audience: lay and ordained church leaders, seminary students, and thoughtful lay Christians who are deeply committed to understanding and strengthening their local congregations. In each case, we make practical suggestions for next steps, particularly as members of these groups participate within intentional Christian communities of radically inclusive, Christ-centered moderate Christians

For Pastors and Lay Church Leaders

As Jacks and Jills of all trades, as the last true Renaissance men and women, you need proficiency in a vast array of tasks. You are the spiritual and organizational leaders of nonprofit organizations that are missionally charged to transform the world on behalf of a countercultural vision of possibilities sparked by Jesus Christ. In the course of a day you may preach, teach a Bible study class, lead a game with teenagers, counsel and care for a couple whose marriage is on the rocks, visit the bedside of a dying parishioner, meet with the finance committee, offer a prayer at a community meeting, and start preparing your next sermon. You try to do it all with love in your hearts and for the sake of the church you serve.

Over the years, most lay and ordained pastors become well-rounded professionals who can manage the majority of their tasks fairly well. There is satisfaction in that kind of competence. But myriad ministerial demands can also make them feel as though they are doing nothing particularly well. The apparent lack of change in congregations and church members can make them feel as though their best efforts amount to no more than institutional maintenance and life-cycle support. Their best and brightest ideas fail to inspire the congregation to make a real difference and after a while they can get jaded. They smile knowingly at the enthusiasm of young ministers and wonder how long it will take before that enthusiasm is ground down by frustrating church conflict and the stubborn refusal of parishioners to take their faith with life-changing seriousness. As careers go, this one is a strange mix of deep satisfaction and endless discouragement.

At the end of the day, when the pace hopefully slows a bit, pastors may reach for a church press magazine that confidently proclaims to us the one hundred and one ways we can be successful leaders of high-impact churches that appeal to thousands of churched and unchurched souls. Every Christian periodical seems to herald the fast growing, media-savvy, dynamic megachurches that most pastors do not and will not serve. However, as they flip through the glossy pages that describe "how you too can have four thousand people at worship on Sunday morning," their hearts may flutter a bit. The eagerness rises up again and momentarily overcomes perpetual discouragement. Maybe if they had a contemporary worship service? Maybe if they replaced the organ with a rock band? Maybe if they were a church of small groups? Maybe if they converted the old church committees to ministry teams? Maybe if they were to attend a Willow Creek seminar to learn how megachurches work? Maybe they could grow their churches too, and become the influential pastors many of them always dreamed of being.

This tangle of satisfaction, discouragement, and longing can be exhausting after a while. We believe that the most important tasks of ministry are caring acts, insightful sermons, and moving worship. Most pastors are devoted to that rhythm of pastoral care and public witness. But we feel concern that the dreams of pastoral leaders mostly go unfulfilled. We worry when we hear about seasoned veterans who, led by their jaded experience, advise young men and women only to become pastors if there is nothing else they can do well—a recipe for mediocrity in ministry if ever there was one. Most of all, we worry when ministers become so desperate over their fading dreams that they turn to models of ministry that don't suit their temperaments and skills, or that don't fit the realities of their congregations.

If you are a minister who has studied this book, or even just picked it up because something about it strikes you as relevant, your dreams are probably those of moderate Christians with both liberal and evangelical instincts—dreams of a witness of love and unity in the face of cultural conflict and ecclesial disharmony. You need to recognize that your dreams matter. They are not merely signs of grandiosity and arrogance, though all of us are prone to such feelings. They are also the places where your imagination and courage fuel decisions and actions, and thus where you engage the God you serve with the greatest energy. You should take those dreams seriously. But to transform dreams into feasible strategies, you need to understand your situation. You need to set aside the advice columns targeted for evangelical-only contexts and seek out resources suited to your church and your temperament.

If you and your church have come to the moderate midlands from the evangelical side, then get to know the emergent church literature that can help to guide people away from the shrillness of biblical literalism and toward an intelligent and socially active faith. If you are in a mainline setting and treasure its diversity and constancy, then look for the literature surrounding religious practices that can help to refocus identity and increase energy in your congregation. If you dream of a church community that resists both the liberal dissipation of congregational energy and the conservative consolidation of authority, and that makes a witness of loving people across ideological and theological differences, then study this book carefully. Read it slowly with a group of local pastors. Conscript a group of lay leaders in your congregation to read it systematically with you and discuss it thoroughly. If you want more sociological and historical background, you might also consider studying the companion volume, *Lost in the Middle?*

Liberal and evangelical churches embrace more pluralism than most—pluralism of political ideology and theological beliefs, at the very least. This means that they are always ready to burst apart at the seams. So it is crucial for your congregations to know what they stand for—namely, loving unity in the face of difference, which is a desperately needed and potently counter-cultural witness to the power of divine love. Most congregations will take their cues about what they stand for as a community from you, their lay and ordained leaders. You need to educate yourself about why this sort of witness matters, what makes it difficult in our context, and how to make it real in a Christian community. That will take work.

The renewal of faith in our time requires moderate Christians to realize that they have an opportunity to be radical in a way that Christians on the extremes do not—radical in their inclusiveness, in their moral witness, and in their communal manifestation of the unifying power of human love in the ambit of divine love. Your people are counting on you to teach them what this means and how to move into that adventure of faith. What sort of example do you need to set?

Liberal and evangelical pastors know it's not about the size, it's about the Spirit. Successful church is not about how many people come forward for an altar call, but how people follow Christ and live out their Christian faith. A growing church is measured primarily not by how many people embrace a particular doctrine, but by how the community embraces the great diversity of God's children. Liberal and evangelical pastors care deeply about mission and Christian education. They are as passionate about Jesus Christ as they are about peace and justice. They welcome and embrace their enemies as well as their friends. Liberal and evangelical pastors stand up for what they believe, but they don't trample people underfoot to make their point. Liberal and evangelical pastors have found compelling ways to love Jesus, while at the same time loving Jesus's friends, no matter how different they may seem to be.

Moderate pastors and churches can build the resources needed to thrive in our twenty-first-century context. They deliberately and faithfully follow Jesus Christ, welcome all people as a beloved children of God, and remember that no one church or faith understands all there is to know about God. We see this happening in liberal and evangelical churches around the country. Liberal and evangelical pastors and lay leaders do not get lost in the middle. They make their home in the middle. And it is in the middle that their most precious dreams about ministry and Christian service can flourish. This can happen for you, just as it has happened for us and for so many other devoted church leaders.

FOR SEMINARIANS

As a seminary student, you have made a commitment to educate yourself in a profound way about the Christian faith. This is an incredibly important decision that will permanently change your life. Some of you may be heading toward ordained ministry and others to lay leadership in the church. Some of you are seeking illumination about your faith and feel quite uncertain about where you stand on moral and theological questions. In fact, if you felt certain about what you think before you came to seminary, it is likely that you feel less certain now. There is something quite disorienting about arriving in a seminary context, equipped with the spiritual perspective of your home congregation, only to find that there is a wide, wide world of Christians out there, past and present, near and far. Most likely, your seminary is quite diverse in culture and opinion, politics and theology. It is easy to feel lost in the middle of an ocean of diverse opinions, particularly when you are a moderate who senses some value in sharply articulated viewpoints of almost all types.

There is a rumor about seminaries that we want to debunk. We mentioned it in the "seminary journey" story of chapter 1. It is an interesting rumor because it has just enough truth to make it plausible, because it plays on seminarians's fears in such a clever way, and because it makes seminary professors seem intimidating in a most amusing way. The rumor is this: going to seminary destroys your faith. But it just isn't so.

The book of Job talks about veins of gold, magnificent jewels, and precious ores buried in the earth (Job 28:1–22). In the same way, the knowledge of God is buried deeply. Some human beings have the curiosity to go for the gold, to search after the wisdom and knowledge of divine things. Seminary is for people who have heard the call to join the quest, to go after the wisdom and knowledge of God that most people never know. Seminary is for mining and refining. It is a time for beautiful gems of wisdom, for precious metals of knowledge, for the excitement of the quest after God. To use the imagery of C. S. Lewis, seminary is a time for children in carefree trust to chase a great and dangerous lion across the fields, to roll with the wondrous beast in the flowers, to laugh with the joy of sacred knowledge, to become wise beyond youthful years while tumbling in happy surrender among the velveted claws and gentle fangs of the one who also holds our hearts.

Don't impugn this wonderful vision of questing after and with God by succumbing to easy rumors. In fact, we would go so far as to say that the faith-destruction seminary rumor has a demonic side: we use it to protect ourselves from the adventure of discovery, to hide from the marvelous perplexities of divine wisdom, to minimize the risk of putting our faith in God more deeply than we ever did before. It's a natural human response. Ezekiel had it right: "When terror comes, they will seek peace, but there will be none. Calamity upon calamity will come, and rumor upon rumor. They will try to get a vision from the prophet; the teaching of the law by the priest will be lost, as will the counsel of the elders." (Ezek. 7:25–26 NIV) We need rumors and gossip most when we are feeling anxious. They make us feel better even when they are desperately untrue.

There are babies in the Christian faith, even adult babies. As the apostle Paul said, "Brothers, I could not address you as spiritual but as worldly—mere infants in Christ. I gave you milk, not solid food, for you were not yet ready for it." (1 Cor. 3:1–2 NIV). The author of Hebrews let a world of frustration overflow with these words: "We have much to say about this, but it is hard to explain because you are slow to learn. In fact, though by this time you ought to be teachers, you need someone to teach you the elementary truths of God's word all over again. You need milk, not solid food!" (Heb. 5:11–12 NIV)

Are you babies in the faith? Is your faith so weak that it has to be nursed through the seminary years? Are you so half-hearted in your quest for God that you would take refuge in cartoon-like simplifications of the challenges of a first-rate theological education? We hope not. If you are ready for meat and not milk, then give the seminary-destroys-your-faith rumor the short shrift it deserves. Let people see your enthusiasm for the knowledge and wisdom of God. Oh, there are twists and turns on this path, to be sure. You'll have to rethink easy convictions and reject as immature what you once thought to be the height of wisdom. You'll learn that the Bible is puzzling as well as comforting, that the history of the church is devastating as well as inspiring, and that the psychology of the pastoral moment is more complex than you dreamed possible.

But where is the destruction of your faith in all of this? The rumor is a lie, a dangerous lie, a damnable lie, an infantalizing lie. Your faith isn't destroyed in seminary; it is introduced to its own potential. We think you must already suspect that this is so if you are reading this book. If you were intensely attached to the comforts of faith's little league, you never would have signed up for the big leagues of seminary education. Others can play it safe with their faith; that path is not for you. You are in seminary because you are more interested in God than in protecting your security. You are in seminary because you are more excited by what there is to learn than afraid to find out how much you didn't know. You are in seminary because you love the idea of growing your faith more than you need the status quo. You are in seminary because you sense that, like the earth itself, the mystery of divine things is at least partly penetrable and you are going to dig as deep and as far as you can, like the miner who just knows the next diamond is near, like a carefree child playing in mud, like a scholar poring over books late at night.

So who started the seminary-destroys-your-faith rumor? It comes from the same source that drives the polarized religious and political discourse of our culture. It is an anxious expression of fear of the Other, whoever and whatever that might be. If you are blessed with both liberal and evangelical instincts, then you will recognize the marks of insecurity and fear in that ru-

mor. You need have no fear of knowledge, of learning, of questing after the truth. Listen to the wisdom of Solomon: "My son,
if you accept my words and store up my commands within you,
turning your ear to wisdom and applying your heart to understanding—indeed, if you call out for insight and cry aloud for
understanding, and if you look for it as for silver and search for
it as for hidden treasure, then you will understand the fear of the
LORD and find the knowledge of God. For the LORD gives wisdom,
and from his mouth come knowledge and understanding" (Prov.
2:1–6 TNIV).Overthrow cavalier distinctions between liberals and
conservatives that are designed to shore up insecure Christian
identities. Name them, criticize them, and reject them. And reject
the rumors and misunderstandings that they perpetuate.

This seminary experience can be a joyous period of discovery
for you: discovery of self, discovery of others, discovery of the
Bible, discovery of theology, and discovery of God. Treasuring
the opportunity now will help you better discharge the responsibility that comes with it when it is your turn to put your deep-
ened faith to work as leader, teacher, pastor, priest, and servant.
So next time you hear the seminary-destroys-your-faith rumor,
don't let it stand. Own up to your enthusiasm and claim your
courage. Declare your commitment to both evangelical fire and
liberal inclusiveness. Seminary is no place for timid rumormon-
gers; it is a place for deep diggers and fierce searchers, for adven-
turers of the soul, and for lovers of God.

FOR LAY CHRISTIANS

Your pastoral leaders and your churches would be lost without
you. Without you there is no community. Without you "Jesus" is
an empty word rattling about in the corridors of history. Without
you the church is a lifeless shell. The measure of the church's
success is directly related to how you, the lay members of your
community, love one another and live out your faith in your daily
lives.

Remember that Jesus's call was not to a bunch of ordained
clergy. Jesus called fishermen, businessmen, hated tax collectors,

feared soldiers, mothers, widows, prostitutes, the able-bodied, the infirm, people with faith, and people without faith. Jesus's call was for everyone to follow him. You have as much right to follow Jesus as anyone else. Your pastor, your church council, your bishop, your church boards do not have a higher claim on Jesus than you do. So take your role in the church and in the world very seriously.

What does that involve? Love, tend to, and work to strengthen your pastor, your church, and your church leadership. Help your community to keep its focus. When you sense that something is amiss, speak up and make your case lovingly. Too often when the going gets tough, lay people get going and hightail it right out of church. Church is messy, community is messy, life is messy. You can't get in the habit of running from it because the mess will follow you until you deal with it. Remember, the church is yours and you are the church. Stick with the body of Christ in sickness and in health, in plenty and in want, in joy and in sorrow as long as you live.

This calling to faithful unity and participation can be challenging for liberal-evangelical Christians because we are not always easily identified or categorized. We can become frustrated in church because we don't feel we fit. We are not always sure where to find our place. We do feel lost at times, and it is hard to believe that any of our well-dressed, well-pressed, and well-spoken neighbors in the pew next to us are as confused as we are. But in fact many of us feel lost in the middle. Most of us are uncertain about our faith, at least some of the time. We are all searching for something we have yet to find. We try to follow Jesus, we try to love God, we try to love our neighbors, and we fail much of the time. But that is not a reason to quit. We are aware that we are lost in this life, and we engage in Christian community in the hope of being found.

The first great test of the liberal-evangelical church, and of your moderate and radical Christian faith, occurs when you face conflict and difference in your community. Can you sit next to someone who will vote oppositely to you on the question of gay marriage and still move forward together to celebrate Communion? Can you participate in a Bible study or a faith discussion group and genuinely strive to understand at depth the person who has a different view of salvation through Christ than you do? It is so easy to shut down in the face of such disagreements. But that is when you and the church both lose. Church can't be only about comfort and agreement, and that is doubly so for the liberal-evangelical church, with its Christ-centered commitment to radical inclusiveness and the principle of *agape* love. Divine love shines when you stay connected, especially when it feels like a major effort to do so. Strive for the spiritual maturity to place love ahead of personal comfort and your church's witness will flourish.

The second great test is whether you will commit yourself to the practices that build up the church and your faith. In particular, will you look for educational opportunities within your congregation and strive to deepen your understanding of your faith? Will you encourage your church to centralize practices such as the Eucharist that bind differently minded people together in the name of Christ? It takes work to learn, and it is often uncomfortable to have our existing beliefs broadened and to make new discoveries. But committing to the journey of learning is part of discipleship and it can be incredibly exciting if you stick with it.

If we have a dream for liberal and evangelical laity, it would be for you to know that you are not alone. There are countless people of faith who struggle just like you do, who are filled with longing just like you are, and who desire a Christ-centered and radically inclusive community just like you do. The more you speak your faith, share your vision for your church, and take leading roles within your community, the more room you will make for people who find themselves lost. You don't have to remain lost in the middle. You can be found in the middle, too, and learn to feel at home there.

Resources for Further Study

Part I

The theological perspective of Part I can be explored further by reading one of the books that we mentioned.

> J. B. Phillips, *Your God Is Too Small: A Guide for Believers and Skeptics Alike* (New York: Touchstone Books, 2004).

For some brief and accessible introductions to theology, consider picking up one of the following books.

> Jim Burklo, *Open Christianity: Home by Another Road* (Scotts Valley, CA: Rising Star Press, 2000).
> John B. Cobb, Jr., *Becoming a Thinking Christian* (Nashville, TN: Abingdon, 1993).
> Paul Alan Laughlin and Glenna S. Jackson, *Remedial Christianity: What Every Believer Should Know about the Faith but Probably Doesn't* (Santa Rosa, CA: Polebridge Press, 2000).

Part II

Part II's discussion of the liberal-evangelical gospel refers to a wide variety of works.

> Saint Anselm, *Cur Deus Homo* or *Why the God-Human?* (1094–1098).
> Saint Augustine, *De bono coniugali* or *The Good of Marriage* (401).

Donald M. Baillie, *God Was in Christ: An Essay on Incarnation and Atonement* (New York: Charles Scribner's Sons, 1948).

Rudolf Bultmann, *New Testament and Mythology and Other Basic Writings,* ed. Schubert M. Ogden (Philadelphia: Fortress Press, 1984).

James D. G. Dunn, *Unity and Diversity in the New Testament: An Inquiry into the Character of Earliest Christianity,* 3d ed. (London: SCM Press, 2006).

C. S. Lewis, *The Chronicles of Narnia,* 7 vols. (there are many editions).

Paul Tillich, *The Courage to Be* (New Haven, CT: Yale University Press, 1952).

J. R. R. Tolkien, *The Lord of the Rings,* 3 vols. (there are many editions).

Part III

Part III's ecumenical perspective also draws on a host of diverse sources. You can get more deeply into various issues raised there using the following publications.

George Barna, *Marketing the Church: What They Never Taught You about Church Growth* (Colorado Springs, CO: NavPress, 1988). Barna's research into church growth and marketing disclose how and why people choose the churches they do, and theological considerations apparently do not play much of a role—the "they" in the title is seminary professors.

———, *Revolution.* (Carol Stream, IL: Tyndale House Publishers, 2006). This short book conveys the author's interpretation of the market research statistics he has been gathering for two decades on revolutionary Christians who often separate from church congregations in order to nurture a more demanding life of faith.

Carmen Renee Berry, *The Unauthorized Guide to Choosing a Church* (Grand Rapids, MI: Brazos Press, 2003). This books helps churches understand church shoppers and helps church shoppers interpret the churches they visit.

Thomas E. Fitzgerald, *The Ecumenical Movement: An Introductory History* (Westport, CT: Praeger Publishers, 2004). This book offers a basic introduction for general readers to the history of the ecumenical movement, written by an Eastern Orthodox.

Angelo Maffeis, *Ecumenical Dialogue* (Collegeville, MN: Liturgical Press, 2005). This book offers a Roman Catholic perspective on the ecumenical movement.

Several Web resources are also valuable.

Alban Institute (www.alban.org). This website includes resources for congregations and their leaders.

Barna Group (www.barna.org). This website includes resources for interpreting surveys of the Barna Group over several decades.

Ecumenism.net (www.ecumenism.net). This website includes a valuable bibliography of ecumenism and the ecumenical movement.

World Alliance of Reformed Churches (warc.jalb.de). This website tracks announcements of its member churches and provides resources to strengthen the unity and witness of Reformed churches worldwide.

World Council of Churches (www.oikoumene.org). This website includes resources to support the ecumenical movement and official documents of the various commissions of the World Council of Churches.

Here is a pair of books that describe the transformation to a liberal-evangelical posture from the evangelical side and from the liberal side, respectively.

Tony Campolo, *Speaking My Mind: The Radical Evangelical Prophet Tackles the Tough Issues That Christians Are Afraid to Face* (Nashville, TN: Thomas Nelson, 2004).

Martin B. Copenhaver, Anthony B. Robinson, and William H. Willimon, *Good News in Exile: Three Pastors Offer a Hopeful Vision for the Church* (Grand Rapids, MI: Eerdmans, 1998).

Part IV

Part IV's practical perspective mentions a couple of sources that are well worth further investigation.

Nancy Tatom Ammerman, *Pillars of Faith: American Congregations and Their Partners* (Berkeley and Los Angeles: University of California Press, 2005).

Jeffrey D. Sachs, "Welfare States, Beyond Ideology," *Scientific American Online,* November 2006 (www.sciam.com).

Many publications take up the major practical themes raised in Part IV. For example, on the radical ethical perspective the church should possess, see the following.

Charles L. Campbell, *The Word Before the Powers: An Ethic of Preaching* (Louisville, KY: Westminster John Knox, 2002).

Jack Nelson-Pallmeyer, *Jesus Against Christianity: Reclaiming the Missing Jesus* (Harrisburg, PA: Trinity Press International, 2001).

The Story of Stuff (www.storyofstuff.com) is a great place to get your head straight about how the radical ethical perspective of Christianity can tackle questions of ecological sustainability.

Part V

The concluding Part V refers to literature in the emergent church movement and the religious practices movement. Starting references are as follows.

Diana Butler Bass, *Christianity for the Rest of Us: How the Neighborhood Church Is Transforming the Faith* (San Francisco: HarperSanFrancisco, 2006).

———, *The Practicing Congregation: Imagining a New Old Church* (Herndon, VA: Alban Institute, 2004).

Gil Rendle and Alice Mann, *Holy Conversations: Strategic Planning as a Spiritual Practice for Congregations* (Herndon, VA: Alban Institute, 2003).

Anthony B. Robinson, *Leadership for Vital Congregations* (Cleveland, OH: Pilgrim Press, 2007).

———, *Transforming Congregational Culture* (Grand Rapids, MI: Eerdmans, 2003).

Index